MW00777958

The Dragon Who Burned
All His Friends

The Dragon Who Burned All His Friends

Cooling Flames of Anger
Through Self-Discovery

An Allegory by Sheila Hatcher

Illustrated by Tianlu Chen

LANGMARC
PUBLISHING
Austin, Texas

The Dragon Who Burned All His Friends
Cooling Flames of Anger Through Self-Discovery
An Allegory by Sheila Hatcher, M.A., MFT

Cover Artist and Illustrator: Tianlu Chen
Copyright Illustrations @ 2011 LangMarc & Sheila Hatcher
Cover Layout and Graphics: Michael Qualben

Copyright © 2011 Sheila Hatcher
First Printing 2011
Printed in the United States of America

All rights reserved. No part of this book may be repro-
duced or transmitted in any form or by any means, electronic
or mechanical, including photocopying, record, or by any
information storage and retrieval system, without the written
permission of the publisher or author, except for review. Any
resemblance to actual persons or events is coincidental.

PUBLISHED BY
LANGMARC PUBLISHING
P.O. BOX 90488
AUSTIN, TEXAS 78709
www.langmarc.com

Library of Congress PCN: 2011940651
ISBN: 1880-292-440

DEDICATION

To Janet and Billie.
Thank you for teaching me the power of story,
through which I found hope.

Contents

Preface ix

Part I

1 It Isn't Easy Being a Dragon 15
2 Burning Hope 21
3 Longing and Remembering 31

Part II

4 Ashton gets a Decoder Ring 39
5 The Color of Smoke and Fire 49
6 Learning from the Tides 55
7 Seeing Through the Fog 65
8 Starfish's New Arm 77
9 Meeting Olivia 89
10 The Lesson in the Water 101
11 Safety Tips from the Fire Chief 113

Part III

12 Spontaneous Combustion 125
13 Sifting Through the Ashes 135

Part IV

14 Putting the Pieces Together 149
15 Spring Cleaning the Secret Cave 157
16 Painting Circles 169
17 A Barge Full of Surprises 177

About the Author 185
About the Illustrator 187
To Order 188

Preface

Tell me a fact and I'll learn.
Tell me a truth and I'll believe.
But tell me a story and it will live in my heart forever.
— Indian Proverb

How long have we been telling stories? No one really knows. It is possible that as long as humans have existed, story has existed. Some believe that the ability to tell a story—to imagine or remember an event and to share the experience with others—is one of the defining characteristics of humanity.

We tell stories for different reasons, such as entertainment, moralizing, explaining the inexplicable, creating compliance, and so on. Very often, we tell a tale to teach. The characters in stories allow us to connect to information in a different way—through emotion.

Who doesn't remember the first time they heard the story of the Ugly Duckling? That poor little thing, who had no idea who he really was, was so mistreated, and who finally saw his true beauty and how he fit into the world. Surely, in hearing that story, we were left with a sense of hope for ourselves, a sense that there was more to our story than we could see at the moment. In telling these tales, we implant ideas that last a lifetime.

Anger is a very real and valid emotion. And most often, we are not taught as children what to do with that anger. So we grow up, doing the best we can. We may be alienating the ones we love, or even frightening them.

We may be getting into legal trouble. We may begin to feel badly about ourselves, to believe the things we are told about who we are.

This book is for adults who want to learn where their anger comes from and how to express the emotion of anger without the behaviors of aggression. Inside this book, through use of story, lie tools for managing anger and understanding the sources of anger.

This book can supplement anger management/conflict resolution classes or counseling. It can be used in conjunction with a more traditional anger management book or workbook. It can be used alone, as a way to obtain a deep understanding of personal growth around the issue of anger.

So sit back, relax, and join Ashton on his journey to learn flame control. Have fun!

Acknowledgments

My heartfelt thanks to Rhea Adams, MFT, and Dr. Bonnie Kennan, MFT, for their tireless support and assistance with this project.

Thank you to Lisa Turner—editor and hand-holder extraordinaire. Dr. Jeanine Auger Roose, you started me on the path to finding myself—thank you.

Thank you Dr. Donald Fridley for helping me to become a better therapist and better person.

And the biggest thanks of all to my husband Patrick— you are truly the compass for my life.

Part I

- 1 -

IT ISN'T EASY BEING A DRAGON

Once upon a time, a fire-breathing dragon named Ashton lived in a village of caves by the edge of the sea. Ashton was a large, magnificent dragon with iridescent, red-orange scales and eyes that were greener than the moss in the ocean. His wing span stretched wider than that of any of the other dragons' in the village. Ashton thought of himself as a good dragon—a fine husband, father, employee, friend. Almost everyone who knew him agreed, at least in principle. The only problem was that Ashton had a difficult time controlling his flame.

Sometimes Ashton flared up without warning. He didn't let anyone know about this problem with his flame. He felt confused and ashamed about it. He imagined that all of his friends flared up exactly when and where they wanted to and for all the right reasons. Ashton, on the other hand, had very little flame control. Sometimes he even scorched his fellow dragons. He had no intention of burning his friends or family; his fire just got hotter and bigger than he intended. Sometimes he surprised even himself with a flare-up, because he didn't see the flame coming.

At other times, Ashton knew he was heating up, and he got so hot he just *had* to open up and flame. If others were in the way, they got burned. And though he hated to admit it, sometimes he let himself heat up until a huge fire raged inside. Then he flamed up just because he wanted to. He felt better after a good outburst: relaxed, powerful, and in control. Of course, because he was really a kind dragon, he felt terrible later when he saw the damage he had done.

He felt especially bad about the harm he'd done to his wife, Winnie. Winnie was a beautiful pink-scaled dragon. When she and Ashton had married fifteen years earlier, all the dragons in the kingdom had envied her scales. They used to shimmer in the sun like rare diamonds. Now her once beautiful, shiny pink scales were dull and lifeless in many patches due to Ashton's flame. Her eyelashes had been burned off so many times they couldn't grow back any more. Winnie wore an asbestos robe to protect herself from Ashton's fire, but it was thick and inflexible. When she wore the robe, she couldn't move around freely; it even made it hard for her to bend over and hug the kids.

Ashton didn't like to see Winnie wearing the robe because it reminded him of how he had hurt her, and he felt guilty. "Please, Honey," Ashton often begged, "take the robe off. I promise I won't burn you again. I can control my flame." She usually did as he requested, because she was afraid that if she didn't he would get upset again.

Like Winnie, Ashton's children avoided him so they wouldn't get burnt. They were proud of their glistening young bodies and didn't want their dad burning their scales. And they were inviting their friends over less and less.

Ashton supposed his kids were embarrassed by him. Or, because of what happened last week, he thought maybe the other kids' parents didn't allow their children to visit any more. One night during one of the kid's fireball games, he had heard some of the other dads talking. One of the dad dragons, a burgundy one who knew everything about fireball, had said to his buddy, "I think I'm keeping the kids away from Ashton's house from now on."

The other dragon, a balding type with saggy wings, said, "I'm with you, man. I've seen Winnie's damaged scales. I don't want him doing that to my kids."

"Yeah. I just don't trust the guy," the know-it-all dragon said.

When Ashton heard this, he stomped over to the dads to tell them they were wrong. Unfortunately, he heated up too much inside, and the flame shot out like a geyser, proving they were right. Ashton was so embarrassed. He trudged over to the far end of the bleachers and hunched down on one of the metal benches, hoping the game would end soon.

Lately, Ashton had noticed scars on his own scales that he hadn't seen before. He had old scars from when his dad had flamed up at him. But now he saw new burn marks and fresh scars. Apparently, his flame sometimes ricocheted and burned his own skin. Ashton guessed he was so hot inside he didn't even notice a little burning on the outside. Still, he was surprised he hadn't felt the burning when it happened.

A few of Ashton's friends stayed loyal to him no matter what. But even they didn't get as close to him as they used to. When discussions got heated, his friends hid behind rocks or under waterfalls—anything flame-proof! Ashton often felt lonely and weighed down by feelings he couldn't describe.

Despite these problems, Ashton liked to hang out with his family and friends. He knew he had flame control issues, but it still hurt when they talked about him and his flame or when they protected themselves from his fire. Sometimes he thought they were jealous. After all, he was a manly dragon with a healthy flame. It wasn't *his* fault it got out of control. His fire blazed when someone said or did something that he didn't like. It was *their* fault if they got burned.

After a particularly horrendous day, when Ashton scorched about half the guys on his team at the Dragon Lanes Bowling Alley, Ashton was particularly upset. None of his buddies wanted to talk to him. His wife was at the burn unit of the local hospital having her latest set of bandages changed, and the kids were away at Advanced Flame-Control Camp. So he walked along the beach below his suburban cave, searching for someone, anyone, who would talk to him.

Finding no one there, he swam out into the water, lay back, spread his wings and floated. He felt so sad and lonely that, just for a minute, he thought about floating face down. If he drowned, would anyone miss him?

This thought made him mad again. So mad, in fact that he opened up his mouth and shot up a big blaze.

- 2 -

Burning Hope

For just a second, Ashton lay on his back admiring the force of his flame. It burned hot, a lovely color of red and orange, and grew to be seven or eight feet high. As he marveled at his flame, a beautiful white seagull flew near him. In an instant, the seagull flew too close to Ashton, singed her wings, and plummeted into the water beside him. He surprised himself by starting to cry.

He sat up, still floating, with tears running down his face. *I'm a terrible dragon!* he thought. *No matter how hard I try, I end up hurting someone.* As quickly as the thought entered his mind, another one replaced it. *It's the stupid seagull's fault. If she hadn't been flying right over me, I wouldn't have burned her. In fact, I'm probably lucky she didn't drop bird poop on me.*

Red-hot anger raged inside him and he puffed more fire. As the flames shot out, he felt like a loser because he'd flared up again. He glanced at the seagull floating on its side. Her soaked, blackened feathers drooped in the inky water.

Was she alive? Ashton picked up the seagull and cradled her in his wing. Was it his imagination, or did he feel the little bird's heart beating? He was afraid to look, so he just floated and held the seagull against his chest. He tried not to think about things. And he tried not to feel anything, because it hurt so much.

As he wondered what to do about the bird, he looked out into the distance and saw something bobbing on the water. It was coming toward him. What was it? It was long on the bottom, with a head or something sticking up, and two long, skinny arm-looking things that kept going into and out of the water. Was it swimming? Why was it coming toward him? Nervous fluttering pricked his chest. He wanted to be left alone. Smoke started puffing out of his nostrils.

The thing kept getting closer and closer, and Ashton's smoke turned into little bursts of flame. As it got closer, Ashton could see that it was a human in a canoe. What was that human doing? Didn't he know he wasn't supposed to approach a fire-breathing dragon?

"Go A-W-A-A-Y-Y-Y!" Ashton roared with a big plume of fire stretching out to the man in the canoe. The man jumped into the water where he was safe from the flame.

That would teach him. Satisfied, Ashton shifted so he could bob comfortably in the water. He had just let out a big sigh and closed his eyes when he felt something brush up against him. He flinched, then opened his eyes and looked over his shoulder. He couldn't believe what he saw. The man was back in his canoe, bobbing on the water just behind him. The man's thin brown hair stuck to the sides of his wet head. Crow's feet surrounded his bold, blue eyes. To Ashton's surprise, the man didn't look a bit scared.

Feeling exhausted, Ashton asked, "Why are you here? What do you want? Can't you see I want to be left alone?" Little puffs of smoke popped out when he spoke, but they weren't very scary.

"I was out on the water, daydreaming, and the next thing I knew I saw a huge flame in the water," the man replied. "I came over to see if someone needed help."

"Do I look like I need help? I'm fine. I don't need anything. Besides—don't you know you're supposed to run *away* from the fire, not toward it?"

The canoeist chuckled as he wiped drops of water from the temples of his head.

"I know fire is dangerous. I'm a fireman. I help people by putting out fires. Sometimes I even save people."

"You're *not* going to put out MY fire!" Ashton bellowed. "I *like* it. My fire keeps me safe. Most folks have the sense to stay away when they see it. You must be too stupid to stay away."

"Wow!" the fireman said. "You sound pretty angry. Have you had a bad day?"

"The worst," Ashton said as he turned away from the man. His feelings were all mixed up. He was so sad

about so many things—burning the seagull, hurting his
wife, his kids avoiding him.

He realized, with surprise, that he was lonely. He
missed the days when he and his good friends would go
on long flights together, wing-tip to wing-tip, just shooting the breeze and enjoying the scenery. Deep down, he
was also ashamed. He didn't want anyone to know he
was losing control of his flame, even this stranger in the
canoe.

The man and the dragon floated together in silence
for a while. Finally the man stuck his hand out and said,
"By the way, my name is Frank."

"Ashton," the dragon replied. "My friends call me
Ash."

They bobbed a little more. Yellow rays of sunshine
felt good on Ashton's scales and the briny smell of the
sea filled his nostrils. Ashton didn't say anything, nor
did Frank. The only sound that could be heard for miles
was the splashing of the water against the boat and the
occasional squawking of seagulls flying overhead.
Ashton thought about Frank. He seemed like a nice guy.
And he wasn't scared of Ashton. Frank wasn't fussing at
Ashton or telling him how terrible he was. He was just
sitting there. Quietly. Patiently. Expectantly.

Finally, Ashton asked, "Do you know any first aid?"

"Sure," Frank replied. "I have all sorts of medical
training. What seems to be the problem?"

Ashton waited a minute to answer. His heart thun-
dered. A dribble of perspiration inched down his neck,
into the water. Was he afraid? He tried to push the

thought away. What did he have to be afraid of? He was a mighty dragon!

Finally, looking down, Ashton tenderly unfurled one wing, revealing the little, charred seagull trembling beneath Ashton's strong wing.

"What happened?" Frank asked.

"Remember that flame you saw earlier? Well . . . I sort of accidentally burned this little bird." Suddenly tears streamed down Ashton's face, and a rush of words poured out. "I didn't mean to! I didn't even know she was there. I was just feeling so bad, and I started heating up inside. The next thing I knew a big flame blasted out of my mouth. This little bird got caught up in it. I'm a terrible dragon! I accidentally hurt folks all the time. My wife is in the burn unit again, my kids hate me, and sometimes my friends won't get near me. My life is horrible, and I don't know what to do." As he sobbed, tears fell on the tiny seagull.

As his tears dripped, Ashton noticed something. As the water lapped onto the little seagull, the black began to wash off, drifting into the water in gray ripples. She wasn't hurt so badly after all.

The dragon began to cry hard again, but this time they were tears of relief. He was so glad the little seagull wasn't badly burned. He felt this tender place opening up inside—a place that had been closed off almost as long as he could remember. He looked at Frank.

"Can you help her?" Ashton asked.

Frank reached out and gently took the little gull. She was still shaking a little but not nearly as much as she had been earlier. Frank checked the seagull's eyes and beak. He looked at her feet and lifted her wings to look underneath them. All the while, he murmured comforting things to the little bird.

"It's okay. We're here to help you. What a terrible thing to happen to you." Frank's voice was soft and lilting, almost like a song.

As Ashton listened, he experienced a deep sense of longing. He couldn't recall anyone ever speaking to him like that. The way Frank spoke was so different from Ashton's parents. His mom and dad were proud, fiery dragons, and they had made sure their son would grow up to be like them. He could remember his mom saying, "We dragons have to be tough on the inside as well as the outside. See your beautiful shiny scales? Imagine you have scales like that forming a box around your heart, protecting it so it won't be hurt." That day, he had imagined a box that was thick and strong as lead. He'd kept imagining it through the years and watched it grow stronger and harder.

Sometimes when he was a little dragon, he would come home from school feeling sad because the other dragon kids had made fun of him. They made fun of his tail, which was much longer than theirs and always got in the way on the playground. They laughed at the way he talked. Ashton was born far away from the sea, where the dragon language was spoken slow and deep, not fast and high-pitched like the dragon kids spoke at his school.

When he was sad, his dad would say, "What's wrong with you, boy? Are you going to let those low-life classmates get the best of you? Of course we look different and talk better than they do—we're inland dragons of the highest social order. Now toughen up! Time to act like a strong he-dragon, not some little dragonette. Go to school tomorrow and show them who they're dealing with. In fact, it's time to fire up that flame of yours and teach your classmates a lesson."

One time as his dad spoke, Ashton noticed smoke curling out of his dad's mouth, then tiny sparks and flames. The little dragon started to back away, and his dad yelled, "Where do you think you're going?" His flame erupted like a volcano. Little Ashton dropped to the ground, the flame skimming his back. He crawled to the door and ran away, with his dad's voice ringing in his ears: "What's wrong with you, boy? You'll never amount to anything. That's right, just run away like you always do."

No, Ashton had never had anyone say the things to him that Frank was saying to the seagull. Not even his mom. When his dad was yelling at him, his mom would just retreat to the back of the cave, humming to herself and slurping her favorite drink—Flame Tamer. He had always wondered why she was humming, because he thought you were supposed to hum when you were happy. She didn't seem happy. Maybe she was happy because of what she was drinking. Sometimes, she drank so much Flame Tamer that she would fall asleep and

Ashton couldn't wake her up. It had scared young Ashton, and he'd worried a great deal about her. He spent a lot of time trying to be her perfect son, to make all of her bad feelings go away so she wouldn't drink so much Flame Tamer, and he wouldn't have to be scared any more.

Now, watching Frank and the bird, Ashton wondered whether anyone would ever say those kinds of things to him. Frank stroked the seagull's neck, and Ashton noticed the seagull had stopped trembling. As Ashton was thinking this, Frank handed the bird back to him.

"She'll be just fine," Frank said. "But she can't be on her own just now. The fire burned her feathers enough that she can't fly until they grow back in. They will grow back, but it will take a while. Do you want to take her home with you?"

Ashton took the seagull in his arms, being careful to support her head and avoid the singed wings. It made him feel like a young daddy with a new baby and reminded him of the time when his kids had been tiny hatchlings. He wondered, sadly, why he hadn't felt this way when he'd held them when they were newly hatched. He was surprised at his feelings for this tiny, vulnerable bird. He knew his own babies had been just as vulnerable.

"You look like a natural," Frank said. "What do you think about taking her home?"

"I'm not so good with little ones," Ashton said. He remembered how Winnie had protected the children when they were young. She wouldn't let him near the eggs; she was afraid he would break them.

"No kids at home, huh?" Frank said.

Ashton straightened his back in the water. "Nah, I've got two of the little nippers. But the wife—she's mostly in charge."

Frank nodded, his forehead wrinkling as he listened.

"When the kids hatched, she fussed about everything. She was always telling me to support their heads and be careful with my tail so I wouldn't knock them over and …" His voice trailed off. He remembered how he would get upset with Winnie for yelling at him and smoke would puff out of his nostrils. She'd stand between him and the kids and scream, "You're not fit to be a father!"

Frank pointed to the little bird. "That seagull must think she'd be just fine."

Ashton looked down at the gull as she curled into his wing. He rocked the little bird gently and whispered, "Would you like to come home with me?" He held his breath as he waited for an answer. The little bird snuggled against Ashton's scales, warm and moist. The dragon let go of a huge sigh. He suddenly realized he felt lighter than he had in a long time. In fact, he was happy. Ashton looked up at Frank, who sat in the boat smiling as he watched the bird.

"You said you know about fire," Ashton said, "and you help people. Do you think you could help a dragon like me?"

"What kind of help do you want?"

"Help controlling my flame. I don't want to keep burning everything in my path."

Frank ran his fingers through his thin hair, which had now dried in the sun. He smiled.

"How about if I meet you here next week—same time, same place?"

Ashton nodded. "But what do I do until then?"

"You don't need to do anything. Just be. Be with your feelings, whatever they are. Be in your body— what does it feel like to be a dragon? What does it feel like to hold that little seagull so gently? Just be—and be here next week."

Frank nodded good-bye and began paddling away. Ashton was sad to see him go because he felt comfortable with Frank. He was already looking forward to seeing him a week later.

-3-

Longing and Remembering

Ashton watched Frank paddle away until he was just a speck on the horizon. Then he looked down at the little seagull.

"Do you have a name?" he asked. He waited. "I suppose if you did, you couldn't tell me. So I'll come up with a name for you." He thought for a minute as he stroked the bird's silky, white feathers, noticing a patch of gray on the wings. She closed her eyes and her muscles relaxed. As Ashton watched the tiny bird so happy and content, she seemed to hold so much promise.

"Can I call you Hope?" Ashton said. The gull wiggled a little, raised her head, and blinked at him. "Hope it is!" the dragon said. "Come on, Hope, let's get out of this water before my scales get all wrinkly."

As Ashton approached his cave, he realized he didn't want to take Hope to his home yet. It was too soon. He wanted to spend time alone with her, get to know her, and figure out why he felt so different with her. If his family knew about Hope, they would just make fun of him for accidentally scorching her. And Hope might like them more than she liked him. After all, they didn't torch birds right out of the sky.

Ashton had a hidden cave at the base of the cliff below his home cave. Nobody knew about the cave. He had filled it with all sorts of things—a lifetime of stuff, really. Boxes full of old videos, photo albums, plaques and awards, yearbooks, old files, and letters. Even old bank statements and worn ledgers were stored there.

If anyone saw all this stuff, they'd think Ashton kept it because he wanted to remember happy times and keep track of good things. But to Ashton, they were often reminders of something that hurt him, or embarrassed him, or caused him to not like himself.

The bank statements and ledgers reminded him of how generous he'd been with other dragons and how they had not been so generous with him. The pictures proved that he looked different from everyone else and that he didn't really have many friends. The letters were from family members who lived back in the Inland area where Ashton would have fit in. He loved to read about life in that area and imagine himself there. He knew he would have been happy if he had lived where all the dragons looked and spoke like he did. The awards and plaques were nice, but even they were a reminder that he got acknowledgment for what he *did*, but never really felt accepted for who he *was*.

Just inside the cave entrance was the pack he carried with him almost everywhere he went. The pack held emergency supplies: a fire extinguisher, gauzes, ointments, pain medications, and gifts to give others when he hurt them. The pack was really heavy, so he found that he stayed closer to home so he didn't have to carry it so far.

Even with all this stuff in it, the cave still had some room in the front off to the side. The sand was soft and clean, and rays of golden sunlight shined through the trees into the opening of the cave, creating a soft, comfortable space. Ashton hollowed out a small spot in the sand, lined it with soft grass, and laid the seagull inside.

"Stay here, Hope," he said. "I'll be back soon with some fresh seafood for your dinner. You'll be safe here." Hope looked up at him with soft unblinking eyes and settled down in her nest. As the dragon watched, she put her head down and went to sleep.

As Ashton approached his home cave a few minutes later, he heard a lot of commotion inside.

"Mommy" one voice called, "Penny's looking at me funny."

He heard another voice say, "Phillip started it, Mommy! He was making weird noises!" He listened for his wife's voice to stop the fighting. He heard nothing. As usual. She never controlled the kids' behavior. She was probably in the kitchen pretending she couldn't hear them. *How can she put up with that noise?* Ashton wondered. *A good mother would do something.* And wouldn't you know the kids would be fighting when Ashton had already had a terrible day.

Heat smoldered inside him, growing with each thought. Smoke swirled out of his nostrils. *What is wrong with my wife and kids? If they cared about me at all, they'd know I'm having a bad day. Do they even care about what happens to me?* The smoke turned into a small flame. The hot flames curled around his nose and horns. As he noticed the flame, he thought, *See how much they upset me? Now they've made me start flaming up again.*

He stood outside the door, puffing smoke and flame, not wanting to enter the cave. But he had to. He was late for dinner, and the sooner he went in, the sooner he could leave to be with Hope again. He held his breath and opened the door. Winnie poked her head out of the kitchen.

"Where have you been? Dinner is getting cold." Winnie stepped into the living room and pointed with a spatula at the kids. "Those kids of yours are driving me crazy! Would you go stop them from fighting?" Winnie shot him a withering look.

Suddenly, exhaustion washed over Ashton like a tidal wave. He plodded through the living room, feeling miserable.

"Quiet, kids," he said, his voice a thin whisper. He went into the bedroom, closed the door, and sat on the edge of the bed.

How did my life get so crazy? he thought. He was so alone. No one understood him. He sat and thought

about his life. He thought about how he didn't feel safe
with anyone. And, apparently, no one felt safe with him.
After a while, he didn't want to think any more. He lay
down on the quilted bedspread. He started to doze off,
but a feeling kept nagging at him, like he was forgetting
something. What was it? It couldn't be very important if
he couldn't remember. He decided not to worry about
it. He fluffed his pillow and thought about how badly
his life had turned out.

Then it hit him. Hope! He bolted upright. He ran out
the back door and down to the sea. He caught a few sand
crabs and minnows and rushed over to see his new
friend. He stopped outside the cave entrance. *What if she
isn't inside? Maybe she's figured out she'd be safer somewhere else. Maybe she knows I'm a lousy dragon,* Ashton
thought. *Maybe …*

His heart pounded so hard it felt like it would leap
out of his chest. He had the urge to run away. But what
if Hope was still in there? She would be hungry by now.
He took a deep breath, squared his shoulders, folded his
wings as nicely as he could, and poked his head in the
opening.

"Hope?" he whispered. "Are you still here?" He
heard a rustling in the corner. As his eyes adjusted to the
dark, he could just make her out in the corner where he
had left her. He went limp with relief. He didn't know
what he would have done if she weren't there; he needed
Hope so much right now. He went over and arranged
the crabs and minnows in front of her, their salty scent
stinging his nostrils.

Hope gobbled the food, then looked up at Ashton. She tilted her head and gazed at him with one gray eye. He could tell that she wanted something, but he had no idea what. Her nest looked fine. He was sure he had brought enough food for such a little bird. What could she want? He sat down and leaned against the wall. He closed his eyes and tried to guess what she wanted.

He felt the slightest nudge against his leg. He opened his eyes and saw that Hope had come out of her nest to lie next to him. Her head was down, and it looked like she was going to sleep. He stayed as still as he could. He didn't want to wake her. She was so tiny, and he was so big. But inside, he didn't feel big. He felt small and fragile, and another feeling he couldn't remember experiencing before: he felt *content*.

Part II

- 4 -

Ashton's Decoder Ring

A week had passed since Ashton had taken Hope to his cave. She was healing nicely, although she was still unable to fly. On the day before he was supposed to meet again with Frank, Ashton went down to the cave as usual to check on Hope. Just as he poked his head through the opening, a small voice inside said, "Hello, Ashton." Startled, Ashton banged his head on the entrance to the cave. "I'm sorry," Hope said. "I didn't mean to frighten you."

Ashton was so surprised! He never knew seagulls could talk—he'd only heard them squawk. He sat down, staring at Hope and rubbing the newly-formed bump on his head. When he got over his shock, he began to chat with her.

"Why can you talk when other seagulls can't?"

Hope cocked her head and looked at him out of one wise eye.

"Ashton, we all talk. But all you could hear was squawking because your heart was closed. You have to open it up to really hear what others are saying."

The thought blew Ashton away. What else had he been missing? He had always assumed that dragons were the smartest and most important of creatures—after all, they were some of the biggest and the only ones who could shoot flames out of their mouths. He had a feeling he was going to learn a lot from Hope. The world was beginning to hold the promise of interesting things to come.

Now, as he prepared to meet with Frank, Ashton realized that he wanted to meet with Frank, but he was feeling strange, too. He had cried in front of Frank. He—Ashton, the big, fierce dragon—did not cry in front of anyone. Actually, he rarely cried at all.

Frank had asked him to pay attention to how he felt. Ashton had tried to do this. But all he knew was that he was either angry or tired most of the time. On the way to meet Frank, Ashton stopped to see if Hope wanted to come with him.

"Not this time," Hope said. "I think you and Frank need to spend some time alone. This is about Frank helping you learn flame control. I would just be a distraction."

A much-wanted distraction, he thought. He said goodbye and headed out to the water.

When he reached the water's edge, he could see Frank's canoe floating in the ocean. Suddenly, he felt nervous. He wanted to leave. He wondered if Frank had seen him. Maybe not. Maybe he could turn around and make a fast getaway. After all, he had a lot of stuff to do today. Why did he want to waste his time with Frank anyway? What could a little fireman like Frank possibly teach the mighty Ashton?

Ashton hesitated, his heart pounding in his chest. He thought back to last week, when he first met the fireman. He remembered how comfortable he had felt with Frank. He remembered the longing he felt while Frank was talking to Hope. He spread his wings and flew out to meet Frank. He remembered why he really wanted to meet with Frank. He wanted to be with someone who wasn't afraid of him, who didn't pretend to like him, who didn't tease him, or tell him all the things that were wrong with him. When he was with Frank, he liked himself just a little bit more. The idea of learning flame control was just a bonus.

He landed a few feet from Frank, being sure not to create a wave that would rock the small canoe. Frank smiled up at him.

"Good morning, my friend! I'm so glad to see you," Frank said. Ashton was surprised to realize that Frank meant it.

"Frank, I'm glad to see you, too."

"How's your week been?" Frank's canoe bobbed in the blue-green water like a toy in a bathtub.

Ashton filled him in on the details of the week—more accidental burnings, the usual feeling of being unwelcome in his own home, and so on. He also told Frank that his in-laws were here to help out with the kids while his wife went in for some cosmetic surgery. There was a new procedure that was supposed to help her scarred scales become shiny and pink again. He was glad she was able to have her scales fixed, but he sure wished her parents weren't staying with them. They didn't like him, and they let him know it. In fact, he had overheard his mother-in-law telling Winnie that she and the kids should leave Ashton and come back to live with her. How dare she!

As Ashton spoke, he started to feel hot inside. Little puffs of smoke escaped from his mouth. The more he talked, the hotter he became.

"By the way, how is Hope?" Frank asked, without mentioning the smoke.

Ashton puffed a good-sized smoke cloud and said, "She's doing great! I'm sure she'll be gone soon. And good riddance!" His muscles tensed at the thought.

Frank just sat there for a minute, watching the dragon and watching the smoke.

"Ashton, I'd like for you to do something for me. This might seem strange, but I'm going to ask you to do it anyway. I'd like for you to close your eyes for a moment. Take a few deep breaths. Relax your body. See if you can get in touch with what you are feeling and let me know," Frank said.

At first Ashton didn't want to do it. What did this have to do with flame control? But for some reason, he decided to trust Frank. He closed his eyes and bobbed in the water. Suddenly, Ashton's smoke disappeared. He realized that he had so many feelings going on inside that it almost didn't make sense. He was happy that Hope was doing so well. He liked her a lot and was glad that he hadn't done her any permanent harm.

He was also sorry she was doing so well. Soon she wouldn't need the protection of his cave. Soon she wouldn't need him. Knowing this made him sad. He was even a little afraid. He'd already gotten used to having her there. He felt so safe with her. So comfortable. What would he do without her?

With this last thought, a tiny puff of smoke popped out of his right nostril. But that was all. He could have let himself flame up over the whole thing. But he really didn't feel like flaming up. He just let himself float, feeling miserable.

"I'm glad Hope is getting better," Ashton said. "I really am. But I'm afraid she'll leave the cave soon, and I'll miss her so much. I don't know what I'll do when she's gone. I get scared when I think about it."

Frank listened and nodded. "What you are experiencing right now is really difficult." They both bobbed on the water in silence. Then Frank pointed out to Ashton that his smoke had disappeared and that his chest wasn't all puffed out and that his eyes weren't such an intense dark color now.

"You know, my flame started to come up again. It usually does when I have a whole bunch of bad feelings.

But this time, I didn't have the energy to go to a full flame," Ashton said quietly. "I'm just feeling sad and lonely and scared."

Frank took a big breath.

"Ashton, it's time to teach you one of the first principles of flame control. Think about some of those difficult feelings. They sort of fit into the categories of fear, pain, and shame. Those are feelings we really don't like. We don't know what to do with them. We don't know how to make them go away. We all have ways of covering up those feelings so that we don't have to feel them. Some humans get angry instead of feeling fear, pain, or shame. And you, my friend, flame up in the same way." Ashton nodded, floating and listening. Frank continued.

"The thing about flaming up is that it seems like it helps you. For one thing, you get to feel powerful. You know what to do when you get hot inside: you smoke, you flame, you roar, you do whatever comes naturally and feels good at the time. Another way it helps is that when you have a good inner burn, you're no longer aware of those more confusing feelings. The flame blocks them from your awareness.

"The problem with this, of course, is that sooner or later, when the flame dies down, those other feelings are still there. And you are just as sad, scared, ashamed, or confused as before. Plus now you probably feel bad about losing control of your flame. And you may have hurt somebody else, too."

Ashton thought about this for a while as he inhaled the briny sea air.

"Frank, everything you say makes sense. But how can I change this? My flame has a life of its own. Sometimes I'm shooting flames out of my mouth before I even know I'm heating up inside!"

"Yes," Frank said, "and it will keep happening for a while. What I suggest, to start, is learning from it after it happens. It's like all the football fans that do Monday morning quarterbacking after a big weekend game. They sit around and talk about the plays that didn't work, and what they would have done differently. So, after you flame up, do this kind of review for yourself. See if you can figure out what you were really feeling that you covered up with the flame.

"Now this is NOT to blame yourself; it's just to learn. Think of your flame-ups as an experiment for a while. Try to become aware of what you're feeling before, during, and after the flame. Pay attention to how big or little the flame is. This awareness is the first step of flame control."

"You mean it's okay if I still flame up?" Ashton asked.

"Of course," Frank said. "In fact, it's to be expected. Because we're talking about flame control, NOT flame banishment. You still need your flame. But you're going to start flaming up less often and less big." Frank dipped his paddle in the water to keep his canoe pointed toward Ashton. He smiled broadly and Ashton listened intently.

"You'll have more access to your feelings and find other ways to get them taken care of than by using fire. Think of it this way: your smoke and flames are like a messenger telling you that you need something that you're not getting. But because you haven't had a decoder ring until now, you couldn't read the message. The flame control methods I'm going to teach you will act like a decoder ring. You will learn to think about the feelings behind your flame and find out what you need. You may need to feel loved, respected, whatever. Your flame is a gift that will let you figure this out. And then you won't need to flame up like you do now."

Ashton felt a curious sense of relief. A peaceful quiet surrounded him as he thought about what Frank said. Maybe he could do this. In his secret cave, he had some old empty journals and some art supplies. Maybe he could write or draw to figure out what he was really feeling.

One of his deepest secrets was that he liked to be creative. He didn't like to admit it, but when he expressed himself in this way he was also expressing his emotions. His dad found out about this when he was a kid and threw out all of his art supplies and journals because "manly dragons don't want to feel their feelings, much less put them on paper for other dragons to see!"

When he'd first left home, Ashton had bought some more supplies, but he couldn't bring himself to use them. Maybe he really was a big dragoness inside, but he didn't have to admit it to himself or anyone else. Now, here was Frank, a firefighter, a human he really respected, encouraging him to feel.

Frank and Ashton talked for a while longer about life and family and just stuff. Ashton liked this time with Frank. Time went by quickly. After what seemed like only a little while, Frank said, "Ashton, our time today is over. Please don't forget about your decoder ring. Pay attention to your flame, and do whatever you can to access your feelings behind the flame. If you can, write about it, so we can talk about what you're learning. And, come back here next week—same time, same place."

Ashton agreed and watched Frank paddle away. Ashton had a lot to think about. His head and his heart felt full. Finally, he spread his wings to fly back to his cave, to Hope, and to his art supplies.

THE COLOR OF SMOKE AND FIRE

It had been a few days since Ashton last met with Frank and learned about the decoder ring. He was so relieved to find out that it was all right to have a flame and to use it. He realized his friends used their flames, and everything usually ended up just fine. So maybe, some day, he could be like them: he could use his flame in the right amount, for the right reason, in the right direction—and everything would be okay. This idea comforted him. Maybe he wasn't a horrible dragon; maybe he just needed to use that decoder ring to get to know himself better.

Ashton was spending a lot of time in the secret cave visiting with Hope. She couldn't fly yet, so she still needed Ashton to provide for her. But she was doing better. In fact, when he was with her, she would walk out to the water and get her own food. She said she was glad she could go eat without pain and was looking forward to being able to fly again. It was important to Ashton was that she wasn't talking about leaving. He knew that she would leave some day, but at least she didn't seem to be in a big hurry. He took comfort in knowing that they would be sharing more time together

Because he felt so safe with Hope and because he opened up his heart with her like he seldom did with anyone else, Ashton decided to try some of the suggestions he had gotten from Frank. He dug around in the back of his cave and found some of his old art supplies. Notebooks that smelled musty but were still dry and usable. Rough-textured canvases that were curling around the edges. Tubes of paint in brilliant red, orange and yellow, and subtle hues of pink, green, and lavender. A comforting, familiar smell filled his nostrils when he opened the tubes. He was surprised that the paints were still good. Maybe the cool, damp cave was the perfect place to store them all these years.

Hope was out having dinner, so he decided it was a good time to try painting. After all, he didn't need to actually watch her eat. He could hear her if she called for help.

Ashton stared at a blank canvas with paint brush in hand, with no idea what to paint. "How does one paint feelings?" he asked aloud to the empty cave. "I don't even know what I feel, much less how to paint it!" A small puff of smoke gusted out of his right nostril. *Hmm . . . now where did that come from?*

He watched the smoke dissipate in the cave. He wondered what was going on. He hadn't known he was starting to flame up, but the smoke was proof that a fire sizzled inside. He struggled, and thought, and pushed himself. He really wanted to do what Frank had asked him to do. And then—poof!—out popped another puff of smoke. *This is nuts! It seems like I can't even **think** without flaming up.* Then it hit him. He had an idea of what was going on, and he started painting.

Ashton lost track of time as he painted. Each brush stroke gave him a sense of freedom, understanding, and release. He layered on different shades of gray. Milky gray. Grays the color of ash and steel. Then he globed black paint in one corner. He stood back. Assessed. Thought. Felt. In a flash, he grabbed his brush and slashed big streaks of red paint across the whole thing. *There,* he thought. *That's how I'm feeling.*

He put his brush down, sat on the floor, leaned back against the cave, and stared at the painting. His mind wandered. He was filled with little inklings of connections, feelings and thoughts, but he couldn't find words to express them, even to himself. He closed his eyes and drifted into a comfortable almost-sleeping quietness.

Then Ashton felt, more than heard, Hope return to the cave. He knew she was there, but she was very quiet. He opened his eyes into slits, wanting to see Hope but not really wanting to move out of his state of reverie. He saw her standing in front of his painting, turning her head from one side to the other, as if hoping to get the perfect view, as if wishing she could use both eyes at one time. She was perfectly quiet, and he could tell she was lost in thought. Finally, he broke the silence.

"I know it's not good. It's not art or anything, but Frank wanted me to try figure out my feelings," Ashton said. "I know it's just a bunch of paint on a canvas."

Hope remained silent, looking at the picture. Finally she said in a quiet voice, "Ashton, it's one of the most powerful things I've ever seen."

"Really?" Ashton was incredulous. "Why?"

"Well," Hope said, "there's a lot of stuff in here. I don't really know what you were expressing when you were painting, but I know how I feel when I look at it."

"How do you feel?" Ashton wasn't sure he wanted to know, yet he desperately wanted to hear her response.

"A whole jumble of things. The shades of gray—they seem powerful. And deep. I sort of get lost in them. And the black—that area is really intense. It makes me feel nervous. And the red—it looks like a big gash across the canvas. The red is on top of the other colors—like that's all that really matters."

"That's it!" Ashton exclaimed. "I didn't really know what I was painting either. I was just trying to paint what I was feeling. And you described it perfectly. I started out with the grays to represent my smoke—I started smoking earlier, and I didn't really even know why. I felt lost. Then I realized I was smoking when I felt frustrated that I couldn't figure out how to do this assignment from Frank. Then I felt asham. smoked. So the black paint was for those feelir. the red: that's just the flame that normally follows the smoke. And you're right, my flame becomes the only thing that matters—the only thing I feel. Frank says I use my flame to cover up frustration and shame. And it all showed up in the painting without me even knowing it!"

Hope rested her wing on Ashton's cheek, just for a second.

Ashton and Hope spent a little more time together that evening, and then Ashton went back to his home cave and family. He felt content, a feeling that was new to him. He liked that feeling. He had dinner with his family, spent a quiet night watching "Dragon Patrol" on television and then, feeling relaxed, he went to bed. Fortunately, he had no idea what the next morning would be like, so he fell into a deep, restful sleep.

- 6 -

LEARNING FROM THE TIDES

The next morning Ashton awoke to the sounds of Winnie yelling at their son Phillip.

"I'm not surprised you waited until the last minute! Now we don't have time to talk about this before school!"

Ashton rolled over and pulled his pillow over his head. *What now? I just wanted a little peace and quiet, and she's in there screaming like a banshee.*

A familiar feeling began to creep over Ashton. His stomach churned. His breath came in shallow gasps. A sense of dread filled him. There was no way that this was going to be a good day. He wanted to stay in bed and be left alone. And then . . . Winnie came into the room.

"Ashton," she said, "it's late. You need to get up and help me get the kids off to school and clean up the mess from breakfast. Do I look like a nanny and a house-keeper all rolled into one?" With every word her voice stung like a wasp. Ashton's stomach developed a huge knot. "Get up NOW!" Winnie stormed out of the room.

Ashton swung his feet off the bed, shrugged his wings to settle them into place, and pushed himself out of bed. A gray puff of smoke floated out of his nose and hovered in the air like a cloud during a storm. *Oh, no, I'm starting to heat up.* Ashton paused. *OK. Frank wants me to pay attention to what's going on. Well, this time I know what's going on. I'm sick and tired of being treated like a slave around here. And I'm tired of all the yelling. I just don't know what to do about it. I guess I'll try to swallow my flame so it won't explode.*

He opened the bedroom door and walked the short way to the kitchen. Both kids were there, backpacks on, ready to fly off to school. They pecked Winnie on the cheek, said "Bye, Dad," and flew off. The cave grew very quiet.

"What was all that noise about?" Ashton grumbled.

"Grades," Winnie replied. "Phillip's report card is mostly D's, and he didn't show it to me until this morning. So I can't really talk about it with him until tonight. He's a sneaky kid."

"D's!" Ashton roared. "How did that happen? That kid is perfectly bright. There is no excuse for D's. I'm not paying for that expensive tutor only to have him end up barely passing. I'm going to visit that tutor today and find out what's going on." Ashton jumped up from the table ready to find Phillip's tutor and tell him what a rotten job he was doing.

"Not so fast, Ash," Winnie said. "Phillip hasn't been going to the tutor this semester."

"WHAT?" Ashton roared.

"I said, it's not the tutor's fault," Winnie replied. Winnie went on to tell Ashton that she had stopped sending Phillip to the tutor because he wanted to go to fireball lessons, and the lessons were expensive and time consuming.

As Ashton heard this, an inferno began building inside him. Smoke billowed out of his nostrils.

"Please don't be mad," Winnie begged. "I didn't want Phillip to be disappointed."

When Ashton opened his mouth to speak, the inferno spewed out of his mouth. Hot, billowing flames filled the kitchen, threatening to hurt not only Winnie but Ashton himself. Winnie ran to the pantry and hid. While running, she kept yammering as she explained what she'd done. The more she talked, the more Ashton flamed. How dare she pull that boy out of tutoring for sports! Doesn't she realize how important an education is? And how dare she do this without talking to me! Ashton wanted to explain these thoughts to her, but all he got out were a few garbled words and huge blasts of fire.

Ashton finally gave up trying to make Winnie understand. She was cowering in the pantry anyway. He went outside and flew away. He kept flying until sheer exhaustion overtook him. He touched down in a lovely green meadow to rest.

Fatigue oozed from every scale. He took a deep breath of the air, smelling the perfume of lush grasses and loamy earth. As he rested, he thought about what had happened, and about Frank. He realized he had let his flame get out of control. Again. It was so frustrating. He was a lousy dragon. He knew that Winnie was a good mom. She did the best she could. Why did he lash out at her like that? He needed to find a way to let her know that he was sorry for flaming up so badly.

A dragonfly fluttered by and Ashton noticed how its iridescent wings sparkled in the sunshine. The purple and pink shimmers were so beautiful. They reminded him of some diamond wing accents Winnie had been wanting. That's it! I'll stop at the jewelry store on the way home and get those diamond wing accents. That will show Winnie how sorry I am.

Ashton was so excited about the idea that he rushed to the store, then back home. He couldn't wait to see the surprise on Winnie's face. He knew she'd forgive him for the morning's flame-up. He opened the door and peeked inside. He noticed the yellow paint in the kitchen was scorched an ugly brown, but Winnie looked as lovely as ever. The pantry had protected her.

"I'm so sorry, Honey," he said. As she hugged him, her body felt a bit stiff.

"It's okay," she mumbled.

"I've got something for you," Ashton said. He held out the diamond wing accents. They sparkled under the kitchen lights, like the dragonfly's wings. Winnie gasped when she saw them.

"They're gorgeous, Ashton."

"I'm so sorry, Honey. I know you're a good mom. I just lost my temper." Winnie's eyelashes fluttered like they had when she was a young dragoness.

"That's so sweet, Ash."

"I promise I'll never flare up like that again." He meant it. Winnie attached the clips to her wings, then folded her pink wings around him.

"I love you, Ashton."

"I love you, too, Winnie."

When it was time to meet with Frank a few days later, Ashton was excited.

"Guess what!" Ash exclaimed when he got close enough for Frank to hear him. "I practiced flame control this week!"

A smile spread across Frank's mouth. "Good for you. Tell me about it."

Ashton told Frank about the horrible fight with Winnie. All of it—the yelling, the diamond wing clips, the making up.

"Since that fight, things have been better than they've been in a long time." Ashton leaned back, comfortable in the sea water.

Frank listened while he heard the story, nodding occasionally. When Ashton was finished, Frank sat silently. Ashton waited for Frank to tell him what a good job he had done, but instead Frank said something that made no sense to Ashton.

"Ashton, have you ever paid attention to the tides that come and go at the beach?"

"Huh?" This was disappointing. And a little odd. "Tides?"

"Yes, tides," Frank said. "Tides are interesting. They have a lot to teach us." The waves lapped at Frank's boat. "Think of the water like a blanket covering most of the earth. During the low tide, the sun and moon tug on the ocean, and the water is pulled back from the land—like a bunched-up blanket. Then, the sun and moon and earth move around a little bit, so the sun and moon don't pull so hard on the water. The water crashes back onto the shore in big waves."

"High tide," Ashton said. "Ya think?" If Frank noticed Ashton's petulant tone, he ignored it.

"Sooner or later everything will move around again, and there will be another low tide."

"What in the world does this have to do with my good news?" Ashton asked. He felt slightly miffed. His great flame control story was being ignored.

"Well, the tides are the result of the influence of the sun and moon, plus wind conditions. If the water was left alone, it would just lie there, in the same place."

The words washed over Ashton. He'd lived by the sea his whole life. He was learning nothing. Frank went on.

"With all those forces, the tides develop a cycle. It is low and calm, and then the waves build up. The tide rushes in, sometimes creating quite a mess. Sooner or later, those influences back off, and the water moves gently back out to sea. It's so predictable, it's printed on calendars."

"I still don't understand what that has to do with how I fixed things up with Winnie." Ashton could hear the irritation in his own voice.

"Ashton, when I first met you, you were having a rough day. The guys at the bowling alley had made fun of you. You felt bad that Winnie was back at the doctor's office. You missed the kids because they were away at camp. And you felt horrible about accidently hurting Hope. Then, when I saw you last week, you told me about your in-laws—that they were visiting and en-couraging Winnie to leave you. These are really stress-ful things. Have you noticed that when you get stressed, it's easier for you to flame up?"

"Well, maybe . . ."

"Now you say that last week you really flamed up at Winnie. And that you felt good at first—it got that fire out of your belly that had been building up for a while."

"O—kay . . ."

"After you thought about it for a while, you felt bad about what you'd done, and you bought Winnie some nice jewelry, and everything has been great since."

"Yes . . ." Finally, Frank was getting it!

"I would like to suggest," Frank said, "that those stressful events in your life were like the sun and moon affecting the ocean. The situation with Phillip's grades was like a wind storm at sea. Combined, they led to a destructive high tide."

"You mean my big flame-up in the kitchen?"

Frank nodded. "Then the stress reduction you felt after the flame-up was like the sun and moon pulling stronger and the winds dying down. What was left was a glassy sea and a low tide. You bought Winnie jewelry to make up for the destruction. Everything seems safe now."

"Well . . ." Ashton replied, "it is safe now."

"Yes," Frank said, "and if you do not find other ways to deal with your stress, you will cycle back into a flare-up, just as surely as the ocean will reach high tide again."

Ashton didn't like what he was hearing. He had learned his lessons and had fixed things with Winnie. From now on their relationship would be like it was in the beginning. And yet what Frank said made sense. Ashton bobbed on the water and let the warm sunshine wash across his face. He didn't like what Frank was saying, yet he knew it was the truth.

"So what can I do when my life gets complicated again? How can I keep my stress down so that I don't have another flare-up?" he finally asked.

"That," Frank said, "is what we are working on. It is not an easy process, nor a fast one. But if you stick with it, it will work."

"I'll do anything. I don't like how out of control my life gets sometimes."

Frank dipped his fingers in the water and brushed them across his arms.

"One thing you can do is to pay attention to your body. Sometimes your body shows pre-flare-up signs before you even know you're heating up. Can you think of anything your body does?"

Ashton thought about it. "Sometimes a little puff of smoke comes out of my nostril, and I don't feel any heat yet. It always surprises me."

"That's great," Frank said. "That's another piece of information for your decoder ring. When the smoke comes up, try to see if there's anything going on that doesn't feel good. Or if something that happened earlier is finally heating up enough to get that smoke going."

"You know, I'm starting to be able to do this!" The thought was exciting to Ashton. He told Frank about the experiment with the painting and how Hope had helped him see that he had painted his feelings without even knowing what they were.

"Excellent!" Frank said. "That's what I'm talking about. Sometimes it's easier to get at stuff creatively than by just trying to figure it out. Good job."

Finally, Ashton was getting the recognition he wanted. It felt nice. It was important to him that Frank saw how hard he was working to change. And he was surprised that it was important to him.

After agreeing to meet again with Frank next week, Ashton flew slowly back to his secret cave. He wanted some quiet time to try to understand everything he and Frank had discussed. Ashton was beginning to understand how very complicated he, and his feelings, were.

- 7 -

SEEING THROUGH THE FOG

For the next few weeks, things went smoothly for Ashton. He was practicing what Frank had taught him. As he became more aware of his body, he noticed that a puff of smoke escaped all too often. This information helped him to pay attention to how he was feeling, and he was starting to get good at it. Not that he really knew what to do with those feelings yet, but they didn't bother him as much as they used to. He was also starting the habit of going to his secret cave and painting when he was confused about his feelings. He was surprised that painting didn't take very long, yet it helped him tremendously. He didn't always end up with an answer about what was going on, but he usually felt better afterwards.

His relationship with Hope was quickly becoming one of his most important friendships. He liked the way she talked about his paintings. She described how she felt when looking at his art—vivid yellow strokes brought her back to happy days as a young hatchling, dark purple-red hues reminded her of being bold and strong when she dived down to catch a fish. Contrasting blue washes brought back wonderful memories of soaring in a clear sky as it was turning dark. When he and Hope talked about his art, he was better able to tune into his own feelings. Hope helped him understand himself, like himself, and relax.

One thing concerned him, however. On a couple of occasions he had seen Hope walking around and flapping her wings. He figured she was exercising her wings to get them strong enough to fly again. The thought of Hope flying away broke his heart. He tried not to think about it.

Ashton continued to meet with Frank once a week and always enjoyed the visits. One thing confused him, though. He rarely mentioned Hope to Frank. He wasn't sure why. It was almost like he was afraid to talk out loud about Hope, in case it would change things. His relationship with Hope was almost like a dream. He didn't want to wake up and find her gone. And he knew that some day he would. He supposed that he would need to talk to Frank about this someday, but not yet.

Ashton was only a couple of days away from his next appointment with Frank when everything fell apart. He didn't even see it coming. He was in the backyard grilling the dinner he had just caught in the nearby forest, feeling relaxed and happy. Then the kids started squabbling about who would set the table for dinner.

Winnie told them to cut it out. Before he knew it, Ashton yelled at Winnie and the kids.

"Enough of this nonsense! Can't a dragon find some peace in his own backyard?"

Then, without even thinking about it, he shot his flame out like a soldier with a flame thrower. It was strange—like he was watching himself do it. But he couldn't stop himself. The more he tried to stop himself, the more the fire in his belly burned. No matter what he said to himself, he just kept burning. Finally, the flame disappeared and all that remained were trails of smoke streaming from his nostrils.

"Look what you've done, Ash," Winnie said, as she pointed at the back fence.

"Oh great," Phillip said as he pouted, "now I can't practice fireball back here."

Ashton looked at the fence. Or at least where the fence had been. Now a few fence posts smoldered and black ashes blew in the breeze. He shook his head as he stared at the fence. He'd have to replace it, of course. More work and time. Phillip was right—an unfenced yard was no place to kick around a fireball, or have a picnic, or chase around with other neighborhood dragons.

Disgusted at himself, he shut the grill and went inside. Let the meat burn up. Who cared? Winnie and the kids probably didn't want to eat dinner with him anyway. He was a complete failure. After all this time with Frank, he still couldn't control his flame.

Ashton was so ashamed of this episode that he didn't even want to see Frank. A few days later he said to Hope, "I'm not meeting Frank today. He can't help me. I'm hopeless."

Hope cocked her head in that unique way of birds. Her orange beak looked almost like it was turned up into a sad smile.

"Ashton, you need to go." Ashton kicked a rock in his cave.

"Why? What's the use?"

"Give Frank more credit," Hope said. "He'll probably be able to help with all of this."

Ashton looked at Hope. Her face looked sincere, her dark eyes earnest. Ashton sighed.

"You're probably right."

Hope chuckled and puffed out her chest in mock arrogance.

"Aren't I always right?" She chuckled again.

Hope was kidding. But Ashton knew what she said was true. He trusted her. She really was right most of the time. He flew out to meet Frank at the appointed time.

After the customary greetings and polite conversation, Frank asked Ashton how his flame control was going. Ashton hung his head.

"Well, you were right. The high tide came crashing in again, and it was pretty destructive," Ashton said. Frank bobbed in his canoe, listening. After a moment, Ashton continued, "I was surprised when it happened. I've been doing all of the things you told me. I've been monitoring my body and paying attention to what I really feel when my flame starts to heat up. I've even done some more art projects. But I still lost control of my flame."

Ashton gave Frank a brief version of the story, about how Winnie had told him he was overcooking the meat, and the kids were ruining his newly-planted garden by running through it while playing fireball. And how no one even seemed to notice that he hadn't torched anyone or anything lately, in spite of the fact that his in-laws were still there, and his job was more stressful than ever. Frank listened, nodding occasionally.

"Ashton," Frank said, "while you were telling me this story, you mentioned some of what you were thinking at the time. You said things like 'no matter what I do, Winnie always finds something wrong with it.' And 'those kids never behave.' And 'everyone should take it easy on me; after all, it's the weekend.' And 'it's not fair. They don't even notice how hard I'm working on my flame control.'"

"So?" Ashton said in a belligerent tone. "All that stuff is true."

"Maybe so," Frank said, "but I'll bet it wasn't completely true. And even if it were all true, did you notice how you started heating up inside more and more with each thought?"

"Well, maybe . . ." Ashton said quietly.

"Okay," Frank said. "It's going to sound like I'm changing the subject, but I promise I'm not. Look out there in the distance. See the fog rolling in?"

"Yeah." Ashton sighed. *Here we go again with one of Frank's comparisons.*

"Now," Frank said, "I know you've lived here a long time, so you know what's out there in the fog, right?"

"Yes," Ashton said. "There's a buoy just inside the edge of it, and farther away is a lighthouse in the ocean on a rock. No one uses it anymore, so it isn't lit. It just has buoys around the rock."

"Right," Frank said. "Now, if you didn't know those things were there, you would be tempted to believe your eyes that there's nothing over there except that big blanket of fog."

"So?" Ashton felt a bit irritated. Frank's hair ruffled in the breeze, and his eyes bored into Ashton.

"You would be missing a lot. The fog would block your view. You would never know all that stuff is there unless you stayed long enough for the sun to burn off the fog."

"What in the world does this have to do with the barbecue incident?" Ashton was incredulous. Here they were, talking about fog when he had a serious problem to solve.

Frank grinned. "Well, the things you were thinking kept you from seeing everything that was there, just like the fog."

"Huh?" Ashton responded, a frown creasing his face.

"Look, Ashton, you thought no matter what you did, Winnie always found something wrong with it. Is that true? Does she always find something wrong with everything you do? Every single time?"

"Well, no," Ashton said quietly. "But it seems like it sometimes."

"*That* is the fog. Thinking that way, using words like 'always' is like a fog that keeps you from being aware of all the times that she doesn't criticize you and of all the times that she actually compliments you."

"Maybe." The word almost stuck in his throat, but Ashton pushed it out. "And I suppose the kids don't always misbehave. In fact they're pretty good kids. They just forget to be careful sometimes."

"There you go!" Frank said. "That's like the sun shining on the fog and burning it away. You are seeing things more realistically now, and you can see the good things happening with your family. How about when you said 'everyone should take it easy on me; after all, it's the weekend.' How was that like the fog?"

"Well," Ashton said, "I think they should have taken it easy on me. They know things have been hard at work and that it's important for me to relax on the weekend."

"That may be true," Frank replied, "but how has the week been for Winnie and the kids?"

"Well, the kids were in midterms all week at Dragon School, and I know it's hard on Winnie having her parents here. They were supposed to leave two weeks ago, and I'm sure she's tired of the extra work they mean for her. Plus they tell her how to raise the kids and clean the house and generally make her life miserable."

"So there are two things to learn here," Frank said. "First, Winnie and the kids needed to relax as much as you did. The kids needed to let off steam by playing fireball, while you needed them to stay out of the garden."

"Yes, I just planted tomatoes."

"But Winnie needed to ignore the kids so she could try to relax, while you needed her to control the kids."

Ashton nodded.

"No one was wrong," Frank said, "and no one was right. It was simply that you had conflicting needs. You all needed things that didn't coexist well together."

Ashton nodded. "I can see what you mean. You said there are two things to learn. What else?"

"The second thing was how you were using the word 'should' while you were thinking these things. 'Shoulds' are interesting. They are like your rule book for life: they 'should' do these things, and they 'shouldn't' do those things. The problem is that the dragons you share your life with have different rule books. Their rules are based on their view of the world, and their wants and needs, just like yours are. When your rule books are in agreement, you will never have to think the word 'should' to yourself. When your rule books differ, you find yourself 'shoulding' if you don't pay attention to your thoughts."

"I see what you mean," Ashton said. "And the 'fairness' thing: I guess that's kind of like the 'shoulds.' I thought it wasn't fair that they didn't notice how hard

I've been working on my flame control. But maybe they didn't notice because it hasn't been that long yet."

Ashton watched a boat sail past in the distance as he thought about fairness and shoulds and flame control. Frank waited patiently. After a couple of peaceful moments breathing in the sweet, salty breeze, Ashton said, "You know, maybe it's too much to expect Winnie and the kids to thank me for doing something I should have been doing all alone. Even if they did notice."

"That's exactly right," Frank said. "Remember those tides we talked about a few weeks ago? It's possible your family was just waiting for the high tide to rush back in for you to flame up again. Just like what happened the other day. It will take time for them to trust the changes you're making. But if you keep working at it and getting better and better at controlling your flame, they will begin to trust the changes." Frank's voice was soft. "And, by the way, so will you."

"So if my thoughts are really important, what can I do about them? I'm always thinking something."

"Yes, we all are," Frank said. "What's important is to pay attention to how you think. Challenge your old ways of thinking. Try to get rid of words like 'always' and 'never' and 'should.' And when you do use them, catch yourself and change the thought."

Ashton scrunched up his forehead as he thought.

"For instance, you could think, 'Okay, Winnie doesn't really always criticize me; in fact this is the first time this week she has.'"

"I can do that, but it'll take practice," Ashton said.

"Yes, all of this takes practice. Also, you mentioned that you couldn't expect your family to thank you for doing something that you should have been doing all along. Remember?"

"Uh huh."

"Be careful about using the word 'should' for yourself, too. 'Should' can be a club to beat yourself up with because you feel guilty or disappointed about the way you handled something. Think about the desire that's connected to whatever was going on. In this case, you could say 'I can't expect them to thank me for something I wish I had been doing all along.' See the difference?"

"That makes sense," Ashton said. "In fact, sometimes when I've used the word 'should' on myself, I've noticed that I smoke a little bit. So I guess it didn't feel good when I did it."

"Exactly. Another thing you can do is use your decoder ring with these kinds of thoughts. When you catch yourself thinking things like 'those kids never behave,' what are you feeling?"

"I have no idea."

"Well, then," Frank said, "that is something you can work on in your private cave. Think about those feeling categories of Fear, Pain, and Shame. Were there any feelings connected to those areas that came up? You might try writing about it, or you could probably paint it. Do whatever you can do to connect the feeling, and ultimately what you need, to what you were thinking."

Ashton nodded.

"Okay." Frank picked up his paddle. "It's time for me to head back. I'll see you next week." The sound of waves splashing against Frank's canoe got softer as Frank paddled away.

Ashton floated in the ocean, alone, thinking about feeling. And feeling about thinking. And finally saying out loud to himself, "This is hard!"

- 8 -

STARFISH'S NEW ARM

As usual, Ashton spent a good amount of time
trying to do what Frank had suggested. He noticed how
much he thought, or even said, words such as "always,
never, should, shouldn't." He was surprised by how
black and white his thinking had become. He wondered, *was I always like this?*

He had also noticed that his paintings were changing. For one thing, he tried to paint them when Hope
was walking along the edge of the water, looking for
food and exercising her wings. It gave him a good
chance to paint in private. He hid the paintings in the
back of the cave before Hope returned from her outings.

The other way Ashton's paintings had changed was
that they were less bold. He'd traded in school-bus
yellow for butter cream and pale lemon. He now pre-
ferred deep crimson and salmon for bright reds and
oranges. His brush strokes had changed, too. They were

soft, more Monet than Picasso. He'd lost his interest in painting fire and smoke. As he looked at the paintings, they looked mostly . . . well . . . sad. Ashton wasn't sure he felt sad, because that was a feeling he usually refused to let himself feel, but the paintings made him wonder.

Every now and then he would see Hope surrounded by other seagulls, chatting and laughing. He was surprised to learn that, while he could understand what Hope was saying, he couldn't understand a word the other birds were saying. It sounded like squawking to him.

Ashton still hadn't talked to Frank about Hope. He just couldn't. Hope would be flying any day now, and Ashton was sure she had found a flock to live with. It was inevitable. What good was life without Hope? He was so afraid of Hope leaving that he couldn't bring himself to talk to Frank about it. If Frank let him voice his fears out loud, Ashton might fall apart.

What if Ashton cried? He hadn't cried in front of Frank since the day he burned Hope. He had worked hard to be a manly dragon with Frank so Frank would respect him. He believed what his dad had taught him— that there is nothing respectable about a grown he-dragon that acts like a dragoness. So Ashton soldiered on, in flame-control lessons and in life.

Until, one day, it happened. Ashton was sitting at the mouth of his secret cave, reflecting on his latest "discussion" with Winnie and watching Hope stride along the edge of the water. She walked with confidence, her chest held high, her eyes bright. A gentle breeze occasionally ruffled a downy feather. Then, without warning, she spread her wings. She flapped. She rose into the air, fluttering her wings hesitantly at first, then finding her rhythm and beating her wings and rising into the blue sky. To Ashton she looked more like an eagle than a seagull. The rhythm of flight was part of her, the rhythm of freedom. She caught an updraft and soared up and up until she was just a tiny speck in the sky.

Ashton's heart jumped into his throat and his pulse quickened. His stomach knotted up tighter than his grandma's doilies. He could barely breathe. There was so much going on inside him that he thought he would explode.

Hope could fly. She was graceful, dipping and rising, flapping and coasting. Her flight was so beautiful that it made him want to cry.

But now she could fly, which meant she didn't need him. Which meant he would never see her again. Why would she want to be with him, a great big dragon who everyone avoided? The dragon with a flame that was so out of control it had nearly killed her?

Hope was gone. She had left him. But she couldn't have! She was his friend. And yet, as he watched, he couldn't even see her as a tiny dot any more.

Ashton knew he should be happy for Hope, but a flame flashed inside of him, as hot as any he'd ever felt. How dare Hope leave me? After all I've done for her! I could have just left her in that ocean to drown or be eaten by a shark. But no, I brought her back here, and nursed her, and babied her, and put my life on hold for her to get better. And did she even thank me? No. She flew away the first time she had a chance.

Not wanting to burn up everything around his cave, Ashton spread his wings and took off, looking for an isolated place to land. As he flew, he boiled inside. He wasn't even thinking; he was just looking for a place to land and erupt. Finally, he found a small, empty, sandy island. He landed. He flamed, magnificent, red-orange flames that filled the air with ashes and smoke. He walked and flamed, kicked the sand, and flamed some more.

Finally he finished. He plopped on the sand, with his back against a boulder, depleted. Maybe, he thought, if I can find Hope again and invite her and all of her friends to come live with me, they would. I could clean out the entire cave so they'll be protected when the storms come in. I can use my flame to make fires for them in the winter so they can stay warm. I can make my cave so nice that they will never want to leave it.

Excited that he had a plan for getting Hope back, Ashton spread his wings and soared into the sky. He thought he would be able to find Hope. After all, his wings were so large compared to hers. He could cover a lot of distance in a little bit of time. He would fly in bigger and bigger circles until he found her and then tell her of his plan. He was sure that Hope and all of her friends would be in his cave by nightfall.

As he flew, the cold rush of evening air engulfed his senses. It smelled sweet up here, damp and salty. He could almost taste the sea. The beach below looked beautiful with whitecaps gracing the waves like snow on the tops of the highest mountains. He searched both the beach and the sky for Hope, squinting into the setting sun to see if the black dot on the horizon could be her, peering down to see if she was with the other seagulls on the rocky cliffs.

As hard as he looked, he did not find Hope. He hunted for her until dark. He found many flocks of seagulls, and each time he got so excited: surely this must be Hope's new flock. But it never was. With each disappointment, he flew a little more slowly. Each time he left a flock without Hope, his body sagged under the weight of disappointment. Finally he flew back to his private cave and crawled inside. He lay in the corner, resting his head on the nest he'd made for Hope. A tear trickled down his huge snout, splashing into the nest, stirring up a downy white feather that settled on his cheek.

This little bit of Hope, resting on his face, was more than Ashton could take. He wailed out loud, gushing dragon tears, crying harder than he had ever cried in his entire life. Hope was gone. He was empty. He had nothing.

Ashton's fire was gone. In its place was a bitter coldness and emptiness. Ashton curled up into a ball, wrapped his wings around himself, and drifted into an uneasy sleep.

Ashton slept through the night and morning. Finally, the afternoon sun beamed into the cave and forced him to open his eyes. He thought to himself, *I have nothing to get up for.* He turned his face away from the cave opening and went back to sleep. He woke up a couple of times, thinking he should go home because Winnie would be wondering where he was. And he thought he should probably get something to eat, as his stomach kept growling. But he couldn't do it. He couldn't force himself to sit up, much less get out of the cave. He just lay there, missing Hope, feeling the cold inside his belly, and dozing off.

Ashton lost track of time. Finally, he stirred when he heard Frank's voice.

"Ashton, is that you? Are you okay? I've been worried about you." Ashton glanced toward Frank, then turned away.

"Go away, Frank. I don't want to talk to you."

"Has something happened?"

Ashton didn't respond. He just wanted to go back to sleep.

"Ashton?"

"Yes, something's happened," Ashton growled. "Hope is gone. She flew away, and I guess she's not coming back."

"I'm so sorry," Frank said. "I wondered why you didn't come to our meeting yesterday. Now I understand. You must miss Hope a lot."

"Yes." Ashton hid his face so Frank wouldn't see the tear trickling down his cheek.

Frank sat down in the opening of the cave, saying nothing. The two of them sat in silence. Finally Frank asked, "Did you know she was going to leave?"

"I guess so." Ashton's voice was flat. "I had seen her exercising her wings, and she was making friends with some of the other seagulls. She tried to talk to me once or twice about the other gulls, but I always changed the subject. I didn't want to think about her leaving. I thought that if I didn't talk about it, I could keep it from happening. Obviously I was wrong. I didn't even get a chance . . . to say . . . good-bye!" Ashton was sobbing so hard he was hiccupping.

Frank didn't say anything for a while. The only sound in the cave was Ashton's weeping.

"Ashton, I don't have any plans for this evening. Would you like it if I stayed here with you?"

Ashton thought about it and said, "Yes, as long as we don't have to talk. But I would like some company."

Ashton and Frank settled into a friendly, if uncomfortable, silence. As the sun set, they both curled up and went to sleep. Darkness settled into the cave, black and murky. Sleep came in a fuzzy haze, though Ashton was always conscious of the dull throb of grief. The night crept by, as dragon and man breathed in the musty air of the cave. Finally, as the sun rose, they both crawled out of the cave, stretched their muscles, and sat gazing at the rosy slashes of sunrise that filled the sky.

As the brilliant morning sun began to warm them, Ashton started talking, his voice quiet. "I used to love coming down here in the early morning to catch Hope's breakfast. Sometimes I would just sit in the cave and watch her sleep, and when she woke up she would look so happy to see me. I miss her so much." A tear trickled down his cheek.

Frank nodded. "It is really sad when we lose someone we love. I don't think I knew how important Hope was to you. You barely mentioned her during all of our talks."

"I know," Ashton said. "I always wanted to, but I was afraid. I guess I thought that if I told you out loud how important she was to me, it would hurt even more when she left. Talking about Hope made her more real."

"Would you like to tell me now?"

"Yeah," Ashton replied quietly. "Hope was the gentlest, wisest creature I've ever known—dragon or otherwise. She always knew when to talk and when to be quiet. She knew when I wanted her to come and sit with me, and when I wanted to be left alone. And, kind of like you, she knew a lot about me. She even understood my paintings when I didn't."

"I can tell she holds a special place in your heart." Frank's voice was soft and sincere.

The two of them sat quietly, watching people playing at the shore, birds in the air, and the tide going out to sea. Finally, it was low tide. Frank got up and strolled to a nearby tide pool. He stooped down and picked up something and walked back to Ashton. He sat down, putting the item over to his side, out of sight.

"When someone you love leaves you, it might feel as if a piece of you is missing," Frank said, "as if there is a hole inside of you."

"I do feel that way. In fact, I can't even feel my fire right now. I just feel dead inside."

"That is completely natural," Frank said. "When we lose something that is important, we may feel all sorts of things. We may feel surprised, or hurt, or angry. We may try to figure out a way to get the something or someone back. We may feel so sad that we feel dead inside, or even wish we were dead."

"That's me," Ashton said. "I don't want to live without Hope. She was the best thing that ever happened to me."

"You know, you won't ever really live without Hope." Frank paused as a tinge of sadness filled his blue eyes. "Even if she is not here, she lives inside of you now. She was so important to you—all the things she did, and said, and was. All the things you felt with her and about her. All of that still lives inside of you. But right now, the pain of her being physically gone from you is so strong that it drowns out your awareness of the ways she still lives in you."

"I can't feel her at all. All I can feel is her being gone, and this big hole inside of me."

Frank reached around to his side and brought out the item he had hidden in a small puddle.

"See this starfish?" Frank asked. "See this arm that's smaller than all of the other ones?"

Ashton studied the starfish's spiny, pink-orange arms.

"Poor little guy. It looks like he got hurt, too."

"Yes," Frank said. "Something happened, and he lost his arm. But starfish have a built-in capacity to heal. This little guy is growing a new arm. Soon he will be whole and complete again. He will always know that something happened to his other arm, but he will be able to live a happy and healthy life because of his ability to regrow."

Ashton ran his fingers over the starfish. It felt crusty and hard to the touch, but the new arm was strong. They sat together in silence for a while. Then Frank asked, "Do you know why I'm telling you about this starfish?"

"I suppose you are trying to make me feel better by telling me that the starfish healed. I guess you want me to know that I will heal, too. But I'm not sure. I feel awfully bad."

"Of course you feel bad," Frank said. "That is because Hope was so important to you. Let yourself feel bad. And anything else you feel. This will take a long time. That starfish did not grow that new arm overnight; in fact, it is still growing. You will not feel better overnight. But you will feel better. And you will be able to access all of those parts of Hope that live in you, that are a part of you now."

"If you say so," Ashton grumbled.

"Will you be okay if I leave now?" Frank asked. "I need to be at work in a couple of hours."

"Yeah. I'll be fine."

"Will you come out and see me as usual next week?"

"I'll be there."

"If you need me before then," Frank said, "just come out onto the water. I take my paddling practice every day at about the same time, so you should be able to catch me. Otherwise, same time, next week. Take care."

Frank walked away in long, purposeful strides. Ashton slumped by the cave opening. Ashton watched Frank go, his water shoes making soft padding sounds on the sand. He cradled the starfish in his hand.

As Ashton watched Frank, he felt thankful for Frank's efforts, but he wasn't sure Frank could make him feel better. Ashton figured Frank probably knew this, too. Ashton watched as Frank crouched down and placed the starfish back into the tide pool. As Frank splashed water over the tiny creature, Ashton noticed how gentle Frank looked, despite his tall height and muscular build. Then Frank readied his canoe and paddled back out to sea.

- 9 -

MEETING OLIVIA

Ashton barely made it through the next week. He stayed away from home as much as possible, which didn't make Winnie happy. Ashton simply didn't care. Because he hadn't talked to her about Hope, he knew Winnie couldn't understand what was going on. They fought a little about his absences, but mostly they pretended everything was okay. The kids stayed outside or in their rooms, away from the tension. Not knowing where he was and who he was with was probably driving Winnie crazy, but Ashton also knew she and the kids got along fine without him.

Although he missed his family, it was easier for Ashton to avoid them. He was also avoiding work. He even called in sick a couple of times. No one there knew what was bothering him. He imagined the guys sitting around in the lunchroom wondering what was going on. Or maybe they didn't care. He spent most of his time in the cave, just sitting there, remembering.

In his mind's eye, Ashton could see himself walking along the edge of the water, humming, and gathering up small tidbits for Hope to eat. He remembered how happy he was while being of service to her. He looked back fondly on the time that he first understood her language and they had a real conversation. He dug out his old artwork and reflected on the insights he'd had about the paintings and himself. These thoughts brought about a strange mixture of feelings. Sometimes Ashton felt comfortable and peaceful—almost happy. The memories were good. Then the realization that Hope was gone came crashing back, and he would feel terrible. He would cry, laugh, and generally act a little crazy. He was glad he would see Frank in a few days.

Finally, it was time, and he flew out to see Frank. He arrived early and bobbed in the water. While he waited, he thought. While he was thinking, he was feeling. And while he was feeling, Frank arrived. Ashton, without knowing he was going to do so, blurted out, "I'm so glad you're here. I'm desperate to talk to you. I think I'm losing my mind!"

All the memories and confusing feelings poured out of Ashton like a flood. At the end of the deluge, he said, "I'm terrified that I'm losing my grip on reality." With this final admission, he lay back in the water, exhausted. Frank listened quietly and finally responded.

"Ashton, everything you are experiencing is to be expected. You are a real dragon, not a cartoon character. You are complex and real, and you live in a world full of other dragons and living things. You impact them, and they impact you. Hope impacted you in a huge way. And now you are processing all of that—all of your feelings about Hope. The loss you feel now that she's gone. And probably a lot of other stuff that I don't even know about."

"Yes, there is a lot of other stuff coming up. I'm thinking about my wife and kids in a way that I haven't in a long time. I'm realizing how much I do love them. They drive me nuts sometimes, but I'm glad they are my family, and I don't know what I'd do if they were ever gone from my life."

"It sounds like the loss of Hope is causing you to reflect on your other relationships, and you've realized how important they are to you." Frank paused as a wave bounced his canoe. "While there's nothing you can do to make sure they never leave you, I'd be willing to bet that the more you tell and show them how important they are, the greater the chance they'll stay."

Ashton sat, listening and nodding. The water soothed him as it lapped around his body.

"Remember a few weeks ago when we were talking about seeing through the fog, about how the fog was like your thoughts? We were discussing how your thoughts might keep you from seeing others and events as they really are," Frank said.

"I remember."

"Well, it sounds like the fog is lifting a little regarding your family. You used to focus on all the things they did wrong, and how miserable you were with them. Now you are focusing on the things you love about them. Nothing has changed, except your thoughts, and then your feelings."

It took a minute for this idea to sink in. Nothing had changed except his thoughts and feelings?

"That may be so," Ashton said in a quiet voice, "but don't you understand that almost makes it worse?"

"How so?"

"If I let myself focus on the good stuff and really start to feel comfortable and loving with them, how will I survive if they leave? I'm barely surviving Hope being gone . . ." Ashton's voice trailed off.

"That's a tough one."

They bobbed together, enjoying the feel of the sun on their skin and scales. The only sounds they could hear were the splash of waves against the boat and the distant squawk of gulls. Finally Frank broke the silence.

"Are you up for a short trip?"

"Where to?"

"You're just going to have to see for yourself when we get there. It's not far, I promise."

This is a little weird, Ashton thought. *Why won't he tell me where we're going?* But, because Frank had never yet let him down, Ashton decided to see what happened.

"Okay, let's go," Ashton said.

"Good. Follow me!"

Frank paddled toward an outcropping of rocks that created a quiet, protected area of water. Flying slowly overhead, Ashton was curious about this little field trip. It was the first time he had been anywhere with Frank other than their usual spot in the ocean, or in his cave. Frank stopped paddling and signaled Ashton to land. Ashton settled in beside Frank and waited expectantly. Frank pointed toward the shore.

"Do you see that little brown thing floating in the water over there?"

"What, that log?" Ashton asked.

"It does look like a log," Frank said. "Wait here." Frank paddled out to the log and began to talk to it. Then, to Ashton's surprise, the log flipped over, and started bobbing end-up in the water. Frank began to paddle toward Ashton with the "log" following behind.

What in the world . . .

Frank pulled up to Ashton and waited for the brown thing to catch up.

"Ashton, I'd like you to meet Olivia the Otter. Olivia, Ashton." Ashton stared at the creature he had thought was a log. He saw a furry creature looking back at him, with eyes that sparked as if they were smiling. Olivia's chocolate-brown fur grew outward in great, thick masses and her long whiskers twitched when she said "hello."

"Pleased to meet you," Ashton said.

"Olivia," Frank said, "would you mind telling Ashton how you spend your day?"

"Certainly, although it's not very exciting." Olivia's voice had a singsong lilt to it. "Most of the time I sleep on my back in the water. It doesn't take much work, because I wrap myself in kelp. That way I don't have to worry about floating away while I nap."

"Um, hmm," Ashton grunted.

"I sleep a lot. I especially like it when the sun warms me up, like today. I doze and doze, listening to the seagulls and shore birds, the wind, and whatever else is making noise."

At the word "seagull," Ashton's heart clenched as if it were in a vise. He fought back uninvited tears and continued to listen.

"Of course I have to eat, so sometimes I dive down and find a sea urchin or clam and bring it up, along with a rock to crack it open. Then it's back to my kelp. I lie on my back and eat, and then take another nap." Sunshine broke across Olivia's face as she grinned. "It's a pretty relaxing life."

"What do you do for excitement?" Ashton asked. "It sounds pretty boring."

"I love to swim. I'm a fast swimmer, and sometimes I have races with my friends." Olivia talked faster and her voice became more high pitched and excited. "And water acrobatics are a lot of fun. But, really, the most fun is to bob in the water, facing the shore, and entertain the humans. They point, and laugh, and take my picture. I'm probably famous!"

Ashton sat listening and thinking. Finally he asked, "It sounds like you spend most of your time having fun. How can you do that? So much stuff happens in life that isn't fun. And how can you sleep out there in the water? Aren't you afraid of sharks?"

Olivia gave a very wise otter smile.

"You're right. Bad things do happen in life. Sometimes sharks get one of us. Sometimes we get sick.

Sometimes we even die. But you know what? Most of the time everything goes really well." She shrugged as if that explanation made all the sense in the world. "I live in one of the most beautiful places in the world. I have great friends and family. I have kelp for food and protection. If I spent all my time worrying that a shark might get one of us, or that we might get a polluted clam, or that a human might hurt us—well, then I wouldn't enjoy my life and the otters I share it with. I just believe that everything will turn out okay in the end."

"Wow. That takes a lot of trust."

Olivia shrugged. "I never thought about it like that. It just comes naturally to me. I guess it is trust. I'm glad I'm able to trust that my world and my loved ones will be okay and that together we can weather bad things that happen."

Ashton noticed that Frank had simply watched the discussion with Olivia, pausing occasionally to shield his eyes from the sun. As Ashton chatted with Olivia, he was impressed with her ability to be at ease. He lay back in the cooling water and wondered whether he could doze off and enjoy it as much as Olivia did. He was about to close his eyes when Frank spoke.

"Olivia, thank you so much for spending time with us this afternoon. It's time for us to go. I'll come visit with you again soon."

With that, Ashton and Frank headed back to their usual spot in the ocean, and Olivia swam back to continue her nap.

When Frank and Ashton had arrived at their meeting place, Frank asked, "What did you think about what Olivia had to say?"

"Well, I was thinking about that while I was flying back. I don't think I ever trusted anyone until I met Hope. Then she left. So the lesson I learned from that is, don't open up, don't trust—because I'll just get hurt." Ashton tried to talk past the choking feeling in his throat. "But then, I've been noticing how much I love my family. It feels good, but I don't want to let myself know how much I love them because I don't want to get hurt again. So, if I can learn to trust like Olivia, I can stop worrying so much and enjoy life more, and those I share it with."

"Exactly," Frank said. "And did you notice anything else about how Olivia described her days?"

"Well . . . Olivia said she naps a lot. And eats when she's hungry. And she plays with her friends. It sounds like she has a nice balance between rest and fun and the work of looking for food."

Frank nodded. "And how balanced is your life?" he asked.

"Not very," Ashton acknowledged. "My job is difficult. I sell charcoal briquettes and lighter fluid. Can you imagine trying to sell those things to a bunch of dragons? I can't seem to convince them that charcoal and lighter fluid create a more contained fire than one they can start themselves."

"I'll bet." Frank chuckled.

"Then when I get home, Winnie has a million things for me to fix in the cave. And the kids need help with their homework. Or the guys on the bowling league want to get together for a few practice frames. It seems like it just never stops."

"So what do you do when the stress piles up like that?"

"I just keep going. My only down time seems to come when I'm laying low after a big flame-up."

"Interesting," Frank said. "It sounds like you feel much better after one of those incidents."

Ashton splashed some water on his brow while he thought about that.

"Yes, I do. The stress goes away for a while."

"Do you see the connection?" Frank asked. "It sounds like you may unconsciously use your flame to relieve stress. At the very least, when you flame up, you get to relax for a while."

"I hadn't thought about it that way. It makes sense. But what can I do? I'm busy all the time."

Frank nibbled on his bottom lip as he thought. "That's not quite true. You find time to lay low after a flare-up. What would happen if you took time to lay low before a flare-up? You would be giving up a little time either way, but time before a flare-up would be productive time, instead of time spent feeling bad about yourself and what you did."

"Yes . . ." Ashton said. "But what would Winnie say? And the kids?"

"I'll bet that if you told them you were going to start taking better care of yourself so you wouldn't lose control of your flame, they'd be glad. It might take time for them to be convinced you're going to use your flame differently, but sooner or later they will see the changes you are making."

"Maybe," Ashton replied. "But I don't know what I would do with my time."

"What are the things you wish you could do that you never seem to get to?" Frank asked.

Ashton didn't even have to think about it. "I loved the painting I was doing. I'm not sure why, but I always felt free while I was painting. It was nice when Hope would help me understand what I was painting, but even if she didn't see my art, I still felt really good."

"There you go," Frank said. "That's one thing you can do to keep stress under control. What else can you do?"

"I love to fly with no particular destination in mind. I like to just find a place to land and explore. It's fun to discover new places. I also like to float on the water, especially on a sunny day, and just watch everyone and everything. The ocean relaxes me."

"Now you're getting the idea." Frank's eyebrows rose in obvious pleasure. "Do you see that these ideas don't take a whole lot of time? Most of them just take an hour or two. If you fit some of these into your week, and even your day, I'll bet you'll find yourself smoking less. And when you start to feel the burn inside, it won't surprise you, because you'll be more aware of yourself.

You'll know that burn means it's time to do one of these things to take care of yourself."

"I can do that!" Ashton was thrilled at the thought. "In fact, my sales route is up and down the coast. I get breaks. I've been spending them on land, usually in the forest because that's where I find my lunch. But there's no reason I couldn't grab a quick bite and then hang out in the water for a while." A breeze skimmed past Ashton as the blue-white ripples of water glistened in the sun. He relished the thought of spending more days like this, enjoying the sea.

Frank smiled. "Perfect. Now you have a plan. The quiet times will help you to deal with how much you miss Hope. You might even find yourself talking to her, saying the things you wish you'd said when she was here. You'll also think, and feel, about a lot of other things you haven't had time to think about. You'll get to know yourself better. And you will feel much more relaxed."

They sat quietly for a moment as Ashton took all of this in. It was hard to get used to the idea that it was okay to take care of himself and that, by doing so, he was making it better for everyone. Finally, he looked at Frank.

"Thank you, Frank. Thank you for taking me to meet Olivia. I am going to try to be more like her. I want to have balance and to be able to trust. I know it will take me a while to learn to live like this." He paused for a few seconds, then added with a wry smile, "If a little otter can do it, I know a mighty dragon can!"

- 10 -

THE LESSON IN THE WATER

During the week after meeting Olivia, Ashton paid attention to how he was feeling. He took breaks every day at the beach. He even found a little time to paint over the weekend. He noticed that Frank was right— he hadn't accidentally flamed up even once. Maybe there was something to this whole flame prevention thing.

He began to spend more time at home with Winnie and the kids. They had not talked about his long absence or his strange mood; they simply went back to life as usual. Winnie did tell Ashton that he seemed different somehow. She didn't elaborate further, and he was afraid to ask what she meant. The kids were soon back to their old ways of being nice when they wanted something and otherwise ignoring him, which felt normal and good to Ashton.

As Frank had predicted, Ashton imagined himself talking to Hope. He told her how important she had

been to him, and how much he missed her. He told her
he was sorry he hadn't talked to her about leaving. He
let her know how afraid he was when he thought of her
leaving his cave, and how he'd pretended she would
never leave. He even mentioned his plan to make his
cave the perfect home for her and her friends, so when
he found her she would never leave again. If only Hope
had been there to hear all of this.

Ashton looked forward to his next meeting with
Frank. He wanted to talk about how his life was beginning to change. He was fascinated that the more he let
himself feel his feelings, even the difficult ones, the
better he felt. He also found out that his father was
wrong—he didn't feel like an overly emotional she-
dragon. He felt stronger and more in control of himself
than he ever had.

When Ashton arrived at their meeting place, Frank
was not in his usual small canoe. He was in a larger
power boat. It was white and sleek with a gold stripe
down the side.

"Why the big boat?" Ashton asked.

"You'll see," Frank said in a teasing voice. "But
before we get to that, how has your week been?"

Ashton updated Frank on his efforts and insights.
Frank offered a few supportive comments, then said, "I
have an adventure planned for us today!"

Ashton's wings rose in anticipation.

"An adventure sounds like just what I need."

"We're going to go out into the ocean and listen to
the ocean sounds. I have some special equipment that

will let us hear what is going on under the water. What do you think?"

"I'm not sure what this has to do with flame control, but it sounds like a lot of fun," Ashton said. "I can't swim under water, so I have no idea what goes on under the surface."

"Follow me." Frank fired up the motor on his boat and took off, heading to the deep part of the ocean. Frank peered through his binoculars, as if searching for something. Curious, Ashton flew behind the boat. After traveling for several miles, Frank cut the engine. The ocean looked different out here, a darker blue, with cloudless skies from one horizon to another. It sounded different, too. No waves spattered the sand, and no birds or people could be heard; instead, there was the deep quiet of water and open sky. Ashton landed right beside the boat.

"What were you looking for?" Ashton asked.

"Ah, that's a secret," Frank said with a grin. "Let's get this sound equipment set up." Ashton waited while Frank hooked up wires and cables and finally dropped a microphone attached to a line down into the water. He lowered it deeper and deeper and finally stopped. He flipped a switch on a large speaker, and said, "Tell me what you hear."

"Well, not much. I can hear rustling sounds; maybe fish swimming near the microphone. Not much else."

"Keep listening," Frank said. "But don't try so hard. Get comfortable and relax. Let your mind wander. Don't try to hear anything in particular, but stay aware of what you do hear. Open up your mind and your heart. Let me know if you hear any new sounds."

Frank sat in his boat, head back, face to the sun, with a trace of a smile on his face. He looked content. Ashton floated next to the boat, also soaking up the sun. Hope flitted across his awareness. He remembered the first time he had been able to understand when Hope spoke. What had at first sounded like squawks later sounded like beautiful language. As he thought about Hope, he heard something new coming from the speakers. It was a strange sound, like something from another world. It sounded almost like a song.

"I think I hear music!" he exclaimed.

Frank nodded and smiled.

"Keep listening, like you were before. See what happens."

Ashton bobbed, and listened, enraptured by the exotic sounds coming from the water. Low, long notes echoed through the water. The sounds reminded Ashton of a resonant cello mixed with a human voice. It was nothing he'd ever heard before.

He hadn't known there was music under the ocean. It was so beautiful! He was sure he was experiencing something no other dragon had ever experienced, and he was awestruck. As the sounds found their way into the center of his soul, something began to happen. Although he couldn't make out words, he knew he was hearing some sort of communication. And he knew what was being communicated. He was hearing inviting songs of love and beauty. He was speechless.

He wasn't sure how long he listened to the songs, lost in their ethereal sounds. But when he recovered from his shock, Ashton spoke to Frank.

"The music is like a language. And there's more than one singer. They are singing to each other. This is amazing!"

Frank nodded, so slightly it was almost imperceptible. He looked happy, as if he enjoyed watching the excitement on Ashton's face. He remained quiet, allowing Ashton to drink in the music and a new awareness of the life under the ocean. As they were both enjoying the underwater concert, Frank pointed in the distance and said, "Look over there."

When Ashton looked, he saw a gray bump in the water, with water spraying out of it. It looked like an enormous water fountain. Then the bump went away, and something gray and leathery rose up out of the water, suspended for a moment like a prehistoric bird.

"What is it?" Ashton gasped.

"That," Frank said, "is a whale. I take it you've never seen one."

"No, I haven't. I usually swim close to shore. When I swim this far out, I'm usually looking for an island, so I'm not paying attention to anything else."

"Whales are so huge that we usually don't see the whole whale at once. That last part we saw was his tail fin. The water we saw earlier was coming out of a blowhole on the top of his head. Whales have been singing the music we've been listening to," Frank explained.

"No way!" Ashton exclaimed. "They can sing?"

"Yes. Amazing, isn't it? They are special creatures."

Ashton watched another whale emerge from the water in a graceful arc. Even though the whale was big, it looked elegant and agile. Frank interrupted his thoughts about these majestic creatures.

"Now think about it. Remember when I first turned on the speakers and you couldn't hear the whales?"

"Yes. They must not have been singing then."

"Oh, but they were," Frank said. "They were singing the entire time."

"Then why couldn't I hear them?"

"It's like that fog we've talked so much about. It's kind of how you think about things. You didn't know there was music under the ocean, so you simply couldn't hear it. When you started to let go of what you thought of as the truth, you could hear the whale song."

Ashton thought about this for a minute.

"You know, I was just thinking about how at first I couldn't understand Hope, and then I could. She said it was because in the beginning my heart was closed." Thoughts started coming together for Ashton, like puzzle pieces that made sense. "Then today you told me to open up my heart. When I did, I could hear the whales singing."

"Yes, when our hearts and minds are open, we can hear all sorts of things we couldn't hear otherwise."

Frank and Ashton sat for a few minutes, the mysterious deep wail humming through the microphone, the sinking sun warming them. Then Ashton sat up with a start and said, "Hey! I could understand Olivia right from the beginning! Why?" Frank smiled knowingly.

"How were you feeling when you met Olivia?"

Ashton tried to remember.

"I was feeling all sorts of things. Mostly sad. Scared. And strangely loving. I was a real mess. I was afraid I was losing my mind."

"That is why you could understand Olivia," Frank said. "Your heart was open because you were raw with emotion. You couldn't tune her out like you normally would."

The idea jolted Ashton's brain like a crack of thunder on a calm summer's morning.

"Wow! I've been missing a lot. I want to hear everything. How do I learn to do this all the time?"

"It's not easy," Frank said. "You will have to break a lot of old habits. But you can practice. The first thing is to pay attention to the fog—to the way you think that prevents you from seeing or hearing what is really there."

Ashton thought about fog, how it made it impossible to see things when he was flying, how it made him feel clammy and frustrated, how it looked gray and foreboding. The idea of thoughts as fog made sense to him. He tuned into what Frank was saying.

"When you can put aside what you think someone should say or do, stop blaming them for your situation, and see things from their point of view, you will hear lots of things you haven't heard before."

"Okay," Ashton replied. "I'll really try to pay attention to how I think about things."

"The other thing that's important," Frank said, "is to keep paying attention to how you feel. And to what needs to happen so you can feel differently. In other words, it's time to dust off that imaginary decoder ring and put it to work."

Ashton nodded thoughtfully. He'd almost forgotten about the decoder ring.

"When you can figure all that stuff out, you can communicate it to others in a way that they can hear. You see, communication goes two ways. You have to be open to hear what is being said, and you have to say things in a 'hearable' way. I can give you a learning tool to help if you would like."

"Absolutely," Ashton replied with relief. "This is starting to sound much more complicated than I thought it would be. What's the tool?"

"Well, it's a fill-in-the-blank. You will want to say things like:

"I feel _____

When you _____

What I need is _____ *."*

"That sounds weird."

"Yes, but you will practice and get good at it and make it your own. Then it won't seem weird any more. The important thing is that you're talking about your own experience instead of blaming others or describing their experiences. You are asking for what you need. This is open, honest communication. You can tell the listener exactly what is going on, listen to his or her side of the story, and then you can negotiate so you can both get your needs met. It actually works; I know from my own experience."

"OK, I'll try," the dragon said warily. "But I don't know . . ."

"The best way to start is to listen. See if you can hear the beautiful song in whatever is being said to you. Then figure out how you're feeling. Pretty soon it will come together for you."

Ashton and Frank watched the whales surface and dive, and surface again, dark silhouettes against a cobalt sky. Once again, Ashton marveled at their size. They were huge creatures. Bigger than dragons. Yet they were capable of such beautiful songs. Maybe Ashton could learn to communicate just as beautifully, in his own dragon way.

Frank hauled the microphone back into the boat and began stowing all of the equipment. Ashton looked around at his surroundings, wanting to take it all in so he could remember this day. Sea water splashed into his mouth and the powerful taste of salt assaulted him. The sounds of whale songs ended as Frank pulled the microphone into the boat, but the sound of a flock of birds overhead took its place. Ashton looked into the sky and saw a flock of seagulls circling. He didn't pay much attention; after all, he was sure Hope wasn't with them. She must have flown far away by now.

But something—some sound caught his ear. It sounded like Hope. He knew he was imagining things. Hope was gone. He needed to face it.

Then one of the gulls landed on the water in front of him. The small bird's gray wings shimmered against its white body. The bird turned its head and looked straight at Ashton. Her bright orange beak curved in a charming bend and her gray eyes sparkled with joy. Ashton would know that look anywhere. The familiar silver wings and clear eyes filled him with a rush of joy. It was Hope!

Ashton was so happy he didn't know what to do. He flapped his wings, knocking the boat around, trying to turn so he could reach out to Hope. Finally, he calmed himself and reached out and laid the softest part of his wing tip on her head, barely touching her, afraid she would vanish into the thick, moist air. Finally, voice cracking, he spoke.

"Hope, I was afraid I had lost you forever."

Hope took a quick breath of surprise.

"Not at all. I just needed to be with some other seagulls for a while. I tried to talk to you about it, but you kept changing the subject. At first, I was only gone for a couple of hours; but when I came back to the cave, you were gone. I stayed for a while, but my friends were waiting for me, so I finally left. I knew I would see you again someday."

Ashton thought of the things he wanted to say to Hope. He had many questions. He was surprised that he was starting to feel hot inside; why was his flame heating up now? He realized that he was too full of mixed-up feelings. He finally spoke to Hope.

"It's time for me to go back to my cave. Would you like to come with me? Your friends can all come, too. I have so many things to say. I want to make sure that I have the time to say them the right way. And I want to take time to hear anything you want to say to me."

"We'd love to come stay with you for a while," Hope replied. "Let us get a head start, because we'll want to eat on the way. We'll be at your cave before dark." Ashton nodded, and the gulls flew away. He looked at Frank, overwhelmed. Tears welled up inside of him, and one escaped, trickling down his huge, scaly cheek.

"It was a good idea for you to invite Hope and her friends to your cave, Ashton," Frank said. "That way, you can use your trip back to process some of your feelings so you don't accidentally flame up. You can think about what you want to say to Hope, and how you want to say it. You can even practice using the learning tool I gave you earlier."

"Yes, I will try. In fact, I'm pretty sure I can do this. Hope is the one living creature that I've felt completely safe with. I can tell her anything. Well . . . Hope and you, of course!"

Frank smiled and wished Ashton well. They agreed to meet next week at their usual meeting place. Then they both headed slowly back to shore.

- 11 -

Safety Tips From the Fire Chief

When Ashton arrived at his cave, Hope and her friends hadn't arrived yet. A hard fist of fear grew in his stomach and his nerves were stretched to the max. *What if Hope and her friends didn't come?*

He pushed the anxiety away. He reminded himself that Hope had always been perfectly reliable. If she'd said she was coming, she was coming. He would have to wait. And he could use this time to fine tune what he wanted to say to her.

He barely had time to think about this before he saw the opening to his cave filling with seagulls, with Hope in the lead. Excitement sizzled through his body and then flattened out in his stomach. He had so many important things to say. He wanted to say everything in a way that was okay for her to hear.

Hope gave Ashton a peck on the cheek, then introduced her friends. Ashton gave a tour of the cave, showing them the areas he had prepared for them with soft feathers and bouquets of orange and yellow gaillardia daisies, perfectly clean and soft. Aromas of damp boulders, pine needles, and moss wafted throughout Ashton's cave in a pleasant perfume. The evening was filled with small talk, as the dragon and the gulls got to know one another.

Finally, the birds began to settle in for the night. The cave quieted. Ashton and Hope left the cave and walked along the seashore. Ashton spoke first.

"I felt so scared and alone when you left with the other birds. Then I lost all control of my flame. Finally, I just crawled into my cave to be alone. I've never felt quite that terrible before. You are so important to me. I'd like for us to talk about what our future looks like together, so I know what to expect and won't be surprised and hurt again." Ashton was proud of himself as the words came out. He was calm and the words were coming out exactly as he'd planned.

Hope listened quietly, and then said, "I'm sorry you felt so terrible. I never meant to hurt you. In fact, I was feeling a little frustrated and trapped. I didn't know what to do. So I finally left. I agree with you that we should figure out how we can spend time together and still live our separate lives as dragon and seagull."

The mighty dragon and tiny seagull strolled up and down the beach, pausing sometimes to admire an iridescent shell or lovely greenish-brown piece of seaweed, calmed by the rhythm of the waves and the beauty of the moon's reflection on the water. It was in this ocean that they had met, and it was here that they were now finally emptying their hearts to each other. Theirs was an unlikely friendship, yet it was a friendship as vast as the ocean they both loved.

They spoke of family and friends and belonging. They spoke of loneliness, fear, and shame. And they spoke of love. When they finally returned to the cave for a bit of sleep, they were both secure in knowing that they would always have each other. They had made plans to stay connected as they moved into their own worlds: Ashton back to his family, Hope back to her flock.

The next morning Hope and her friends left for a few days of flight practice and food searching. The gulls were tired of eating the same thing day after day and found different things to eat as they traveled along different parts of the coast. Ashton returned home to his wife and kids, excited about his new way of communicating.

When Ashton got to his cave, he peeked in the door. Winnie was sitting in the easy chair, reading *Dragons' Home Journal.* His eyes became moist when he saw her. Marriage was hard at times, but when he saw Winnie with her shiny pink scales and beautiful dark eyes, he remembered how much he loved his wife. Best of all, he could see the lovely curves and contours of her body because she wasn't wearing the ugly asbestos robe.

"Winnie!" Ashton said. "I'm home!"

Winnie put down her magazine and looked up at him.

"Hi, Honey," she said with a smile. "I was wondering if you would be home today. You've been gone so much lately that I'm really starting to miss you."

"I've missed you, too. Things have been a little crazy lately—stuff I'll fill you in on when I understand it better myself. Just know that I'm really starting to realize how lucky I am to have you and the kids in my life."

"Wow! Now that's a tease. Just don't keep me wondering too long." She got out of her chair and gave him a hug. They went into the kitchen to share a cup of coffee and the morning paper.

The week went smoothly. The kids were off to Flame Control Camp, and Winnie's folks had finally left. It was just the two of them: Ashton and Winnie. They talked a little, about nothing very important. It seemed as if neither one of them wanted to rock the boat, so they kept a respectful emotional distance, and no flame-ups occurred.

Before Ashton knew it, it was time for his next appointment with Frank. He went to the usual spot at the usual time, excited to share with the fireman all of the exciting things he and Hope had talked about. He sat peacefully in the water, looking out into the distance, feeling content. Frank paddled up to Ashton but didn't say anything. He approached slowly, rested his paddle inside the canoe, and waited.

Ashton spoke quietly, without looking at Frank. "You know, the sentence formula you gave me really worked. I practiced it for a long time until I saw Hope, and then when I did see her, everything I said came out in a way that showed how much I care about her, and how much I want to feel safe with her. And she was able to say some things to me that sort of surprised me, and I'm glad she was able to say them. Do you know, she even said she had been trying to talk to me about leaving, and I kept changing the subject? I don't remember that at all."

Frank sat, nodding, and finally said, "I'm glad you found the formula to be helpful. Did you get what you needed from the conversation?"

"Yes, I did. We've developed a plan so we still get to see each other, but I get back to my life with my family and my work, and she gets to live with her new flock. It seems right somehow. It's good now that I know I still have Hope in my life."

"Ah, so you'll be spending more time with your family now and less time in your secret cave?"

"Yes. I actually miss them. Now I want to take all of these things you've taught me and use them with my family. If they work with Hope, I'm guessing they can work other places, too. Especially with dragons—after all, we speak the same language."

"True, but it may not be easy. Your family and your friends are used to you behaving in a certain way, such as losing control of your flame. They may not know how to respond to the new you. They may even want the old you back, because as much as they hated being burned all the time, they were somewhat comfortable in the patterns you developed together. So be prepared for anything that happens. And remember that you love them, and that is why all this flame control stuff started in the first place."

Ashton nodded, and they floated together in friendly silence. Finally, Frank spoke

"There he is! I was starting to think he got lost." Frank pointed to a small boat motoring toward them. "I've got someone I want you to meet." The boat pulled up next to Frank's canoe and the man inside cut the motor. He looked up at the huge dragon, and he said to Frank nervously, "This is the student you were telling me about?"

"Yes," Frank said. Ashton and Charley the Fire Chief exchanged greetings.

"I've asked the Chief to come out and talk to you about fire prevention," Frank said. "This is his specialty. He goes to schools and town meetings and talks to all the people who will listen. I thought he might have some things to say that might be helpful to you, too."

"Sure, why not?" Ashton said. Turning to the Chief, Ashton reviewed his flame history and told Charley how much Frank had helped him.

"I'm glad to hear that," the Chief answered. "What I usually help people with is finding ways they can prevent a fire—like in their homes and offices. I'm not sure how that will help here, but let's see what happens."

Ashton looked at Frank, who simply nodded toward Charley.

"Well . . ." Charley started. "Let's see. One really important thing is to watch out for too many things plugged into one wall outlet. It can overheat and start a fire that no one is noticing. Another thing I tell people not to do is to run a cord under a rug where it can be walked on. The cord covering can wear away and expose the wires, which would be a sure-fire way to have a problem. No pun intended!" Charley grinned at his own joke.

"I get it," Ashton said. "Frank taught me about stress, which is like having too many things plugged into the wall. I've also learned about other feelings like fear, pain, and shame. Sometimes things just rub me wrong and those feelings get exposed, and I flame up. Like the wires under the rug."

"Excellent!" Charley seemed thrilled that Ashton caught on so quickly. Ashton reveled in pride just a little. "I can see why Frank said you were such a good student. Something else I talk about is what to do when, no matter how careful you've been, you get a fire anyway. Does that ever happen to you?"

"Yeah." Ashton's pride deflated like an old balloon, and he hung his head in shame. "Not as often as it used to, but it still happens. It happened a couple of weeks ago, but at least this time I left before it got too bad. I found an island where nothing would get hurt and flamed up real good."

Charley didn't seem surprised.

"I tell people to keep a fire extinguisher in their homes. When a fire starts to smolder, they get the extinguisher, and they douse the fire before it gets too big. Then they can tend to whatever led to the fire. You can do something similar. I know Frank taught you about the fog and how you think."

Ashton nodded.

Charley stretched his neck and looked up at Ashton. "So when you feel yourself heating up, go ahead and leave like you did before. But tell whoever you're with that you're going to leave because you don't want to lose control of your flame and that you'll be back to talk to them about the situation. Then go somewhere your flame won't cause any damage. While you're there, pay attention to your thoughts. Think about the situation differently so your flame can cool off. That is like going to get the fire extinguisher and then dousing the flames. You can go back later to finish the conversation."

Ashton could almost see a light bulb flash above his head like in a cartoon.

"I get it! Changing my thoughts puts out my fire. Then I can go back to discuss the situation with the sentence formula Frank taught me, so the problem won't lead to another flame-up."

Charley's face crinkled into a friendly smile.

"Yes. Another thing I talk to people about is how they are responsible to a large extent for how safe their lives are. If they live in a home with really bad wiring, for example, they need to either rewire the house or move out. If they continue to live in the house with bad wiring and hope nothing happens, they're at risk for a fire. If a fire starts, their lives may be ruined. Even if the fire never comes, they may worry all the time. Worry leads to stress and all sorts of problems that could be avoided if they could just take responsibility for the wiring."

"I'm afraid I don't see the connection for this one," Ashton said with a slight frown.

"I do," Frank said. "In flame control, things come up that cause you to heat up inside. Your life is stressful, or you're dealing with difficult feelings, or whatever. It's up to you to practice stress-reduction exercises, process your difficult feelings, and use your sentence formulas to talk to your friends and family to try to get your needs met. That is like rewiring the house."

While Frank paused to take a sip of water from a plastic bottle, Ashton thought for a minute about the wiring in a house. Wiring was complicated. Like feelings and flame control. Frank put down his water bottle and continued.

"Sometimes, no matter how much you work at those things, you may still find that you're stressed, or hurt, or whatever. You may need to leave a job or give up a friendship. That's like moving out of a house with bad wiring. Either way, you take responsibility for the quality of your life, so you don't lose control of your flame."

"Ahh," Ashton sighed. "I think you're saying that if I can't change what is happening in my relationships, I need to find ways to accept what's happening, or let go of those relationships. Otherwise, I'm at risk for an unexpected flare-up."

"Yes!" Charley said.

"You've got it!" Frank's eyes seemed to sparkle.

"I'll keep that in the back of my mind," Ashton said, somewhat perplexed. "I just can't imagine actually ending any of my relationships . . . ."

"I don't think you'll need to, based on what you've told me," Frank said. "Just remember to focus on anything that needs rewiring, so you can stay in your lovely home." Ashton gave Frank a thumbs up.

"Will do."

"Oh," Frank added, "I almost forgot to tell you. I will be going out of town for the next week. There's a big Fireman's Convention in the city, and I'll be staying there in a hotel. So I won't be able to meet with you next week. I'll be here the week after that, though. Same time, same place."

Ashton told Frank to enjoy his convention. Then he said good-bye to the two men and watched them as they left, getting smaller and smaller in the distance. He knew he needed, and wanted, to spend time with Winnie and the kids. He hadn't spent enough time with them lately. He'd been too busy with Hope, and then mourning Hope. He had so much to share with them. He decided to practice his sentence formulas on the way back.

He spread his wings and flew toward home, slowly, to the dragons he loved.

PART III

- 12 -

Spontaneous Combustion

Ashton met Hope down at the beach every few days. They walked along the water's edge or hung out in his secret cave. Once they even flew off together to a nearby island just for fun. The time together always seemed too short.

Ashton now spent most of his time at home. He was actually enjoying the time with his family. Everything continued to go well with Winnie. They weren't fighting, and they went to the occasional movie or dinner together. The kids were back from Flame Control Camp and were on their best behavior. Maybe his family was learning to be a family again.

Ashton was also feeling better at work. Selling charcoal briquettes and lighter fluid was still no easy task, but his bosses had stopped expecting him to sell quite so much. This helped Ashton to feel more relaxed.

Things were even good with the bowling league.

Ashton's team, the Thorny Backs, continued to be one of
the top-ranked teams in the league. Ashton was throw-
ing more spares and strikes and having a great time
tossing back chips and beer at the alley. The other
Thorny Backs weren't picking on him as much since he
wasn't having so many accidental flare-ups.

So, Ashton was happy. So happy, in fact, that he
decided to take Winnie and the kids for a weekend out
of town. He met with a travel agent and booked an
island resort about a half-day's flight away.

Dragon Dreams Resort had everything a family
could want. Pristine beaches of endless white sand.
Great restaurants that were still kid-friendly. Water
parks and pools with swim-up bars. The resort offered
day camps to keep the kids occupied and romantic
spaces for the adults. Ashton thought how nice it would
be to a have a quiet picnic with Winnie, like they did
when they were dating. He was even able to get a suite,
so the kids could have their own room and television,
and he and Winnie could still keep an eye on them.
Ashton raced home, excited to tell his family about his
plans. During dinner, Ashton decided it was time to
share the good news.

"Great news, everybody! I've decided we need to
spend more time together as a family. Phillip and Penny,
you're growing so fast I'm afraid I'll come home one day
and not recognize you. So, this weekend, we're going to
Dragon Dreams Resort. Isn't that great?"

Ashton sat back like a king on his throne, waiting for
Winnie and the kids to jump up and hug him. But no one

moved. Winnie sat there, her lips drawn up in a tight smile, food half way to her mouth. She looked like she'd just been stung by a wasp. The kids both looked down at their plates as if green peas had suddenly become fascinating items to study, saying nothing. Ashton's grin slowly faded away, and a look of confusion took its place.

"I thought you would be happy about this. Why aren't you excited?" The confusion was obvious in Ashton's voice. "We haven't done anything together in a long time."

Winnie finally put down her fork full of mashed potatoes.

"Ashton," she began in a quiet voice, "have you forgotten how horrible our last family vacation was?" She dabbed at her mouth with her napkin. "Have you forgotten that both of the kids were burned pretty bad and that I ended up back in the burn unit?" She paused for a moment, as if deciding whether to say anything else, then picked up her biscuit and took a bite out of it.

Surprise and hurt coursed through Ashton's body. "But I've been doing so good. We haven't had a single argument in over two weeks."

"That's true," Winnie said. "But still . . . a whole weekend together. I don't know. Kids, what do you think?"

"I don't wanna go," Penny whined, her young horns bouncing as she shook her head. "There won't be anything to do there."

"Me either," Phillip chimed in. "It sounds boring."

Ashton could feel himself heating up inside. Ingrates! They didn't know what they were talking about. He had made sure to find a resort with lots of entertainment for the kids. He shot Winnie a withering look.

"The kids don't get to decide what we do. I want to go. So we are going!" Ashton stood up, his clenched fists at his side, and he stormed into the family room. He snapped on the television and the sounds of "Dragon Idol" filled the room, giving a clear message that the discussion was over.

The rest of the night was chilly in the Mondragon household. Phillip and Penny scuttled to their rooms and played video games. Winnie sat outside and pretended to read a book. Ashton slept fitfully in front of the blaring television set.

The next day, all Ashton could think of was his family's reaction to his good news. What in the world was wrong with them? Any other family would be thrilled to take this trip. The more he thought about it, the more he felt himself heating up. Still, Ashton was sure he could control his flame once he got to the island. He could hit the beach and relax. So could Winnie and the kids. He knew they would enjoy it. When he got home that evening, he made sure everyone was packed and ready to leave first thing the next morning.

When morning came, Ashton woke everyone up before dawn. "Dad," Phillip whimpered, "it's still dark."

"Honey, do we need to leave this early?" Winnie's voice was low and clogged with sleep.

"Check-in is at noon, and it will take us several hours to get there. I want to get our money's worth. So, get up and get going."

The family stumbled out of their beds and got ready fairly quickly. Ashton took the lead on the flight with Winnie, Penny and Phillip close behind. As he flew, Ashton began to feel hopeful again. Surely, once they saw how beautiful this resort was, everyone would be excited.

They arrived at the island a little before lunch. They oriented themselves and found the office for check-in. Ashton went up to the desk clerk, a skinny green dragon wearing wire-rimmed glasses on his bony face.

"I'm Ashton Mondragon, and I have a reservation for a suite." The clerk clicked on a computer, adjusted his glasses and looked up.

"I'm sorry, Mr. Mondragon. The current occupant has been ill and won't be checking out until a room is available at the infirmary. It could be as late as dinner time before your room is ready."

Heat simmered inside Ashton; then he caught himself. He took a deep breath, checked his flame to make sure it wouldn't pop out, and spoke in his most well-mannered voice.

"Well, that is very unfortunate. I am sorry your guest is ill. Do you have somewhere to store our luggage while we wait for our room?"

"Of course," the clerk replied. "Thank you for being so understanding. I would like to offer your family complimentary lunch at any restaurant you choose while you wait for your room."

"Splendid!" Ashton felt simultaneously proud he had handled the situation without flaming up and nervous about telling the family that they were without a room for a few hours. When he told Winnie and the kids about the free lunch, they picked the most expensive restaurant on the island and decided that things could be worse. After all, it's hard to be too upset when eating free food.

The family ate a delicious lunch of steak and potatoes and explored the island until the room was ready. When they finally got to the room, Winnie and Ashton settled into the large room, and the kids went into the smaller room.

"Wow! A TV and video games! Maybe this won't be such a bad trip after all!" Phillip exclaimed.

Penny squealed with delight as she flopped on the red bedspread.

"I can watch 'Dancing Dragonettes' all afternoon!"

"Oh, no, you're not!" Phillip said, as he planted himself on the other bed in the room. "No way am I watching dumb ol' 'Dancing Dragonettes' when I could be playing Reptilian Racing!"

So it began. The kids, who got along fairly well at home, alternated between yelling, whining, and crying. They bickered about television shows, screamed about games, and bellyached about everything. Before long, everyone was miserable.

Ashton could not understand why Winnie just let them go on instead of jumping in and putting an end to their squabbles. But, he had promised everyone he would not flame up, so he spoke in the calmest voice he could muster.

"Winnie, would you please help the kids develop a schedule for themselves so they don't fight the whole night?"

"I'd rather let them learn to work it out themselves," Winnie said. "Just ignore them." This irritated Ashton, but he clamped his mouth shut. *Don't rock the boat,* he thought.

Finally it was time to go down for dinner. The restaurant was a casual eatery with curly fries, burgers, and hot dogs for the kids and elegant pasta dishes for the adults. Light bounced off bright coral and blue walls while sea breezes fanned the diners. Night blooming jasmine perfumed the air. The kids tucked into their burgers and finished them quickly. As Winnie and Ashton nibbled their fettuccini carbonara, Penny spoke up.

"This is boring. Why don't they have a TV here?"

"Yea," Phillip agreed. "I like watching TV while we eat, like we do at home."

Winnie shot them a withering look, but the kids kept up the complaints while poking each other with French fries. Again, Ashton felt the fire smoldering inside, but he decided to say nothing and tried to tolerate the fidgety kids.

When they got back to the suite, Ashton put the kids in their room and closed the door so he couldn't hear them arguing. Relieved to be away from them, he went over to Winnie.

"How about we find an old movie and snuggle on the couch like we used to?" He put his arm around her and squeezed her tightly. "I've missed being with you," he whispered in her ear. He could feel Winnie stiffen up. She didn't say anything, but she went to the couch and sat down.

"Whatever you would like, dear." Her voice sounded starchy and artificial.

Ashton was confused. Didn't she want to watch a movie with him? Hadn't she missed him, too? They'd been getting along so well. Wasn't some cozy time together the next step?

Maybe not. For the first time, a terrible thought blasted into Ashton's consciousness. Maybe Winnie didn't care. For all he knew, she'd been glad he had been with Hope so much. Maybe she was disappointed that he was home more now. Flames licked at his throat, and he felt smoke curling around inside.

Ashton pushed the flame down and sat beside Winnie, flipping through the channels until he came upon an old classic. *Casablanca*. What could be better? He wanted to put his arm around Winnie, but his arm felt wooden and he couldn't bring himself to do it. Winnie sat up straight on her side of the couch, prim as a librarian. When the movie ended, they checked on the kids and went to bed without saying a word.

The next morning Ashton announced to the family that he wanted them all to take a long hike to the middle of the island after breakfast.

"Sweetie, I just had my nails done for this trip." Winnie held up her shiny crimson nails. "I don't want to mess them up. I'd rather go have a massage and scale-polishing."

"Hiking is boring. I want to go hunting in the forest," Phillip said.

"I hate to hike. I want to go swimming. I never get to swim at home," Penny said in a whining voice. "This trip is stupid!" Then Penny started crying.

Winnie rushed over to Penny and put her arm around her small shoulders.

"It's okay, dear. You don't have to go hiking. Please don't cry. It makes Mommy sad to see you cry." Winnie stretched out her other arm and scooped Phillip close to her. "We can sign you up for a hunting trip. You don't have to go hiking if you don't want to."

Ashton looked at his wife, with her arms around her kids, comfy and affectionate. They looked like . . . a family. Suddenly he felt completely alone. He was the odd-dragon out. He had no place in his own family. He opened his mouth to say, "You don't have to go with me if you don't want to. I'll just go by myself." But that was not what happened.

When he opened his mouth, a big flame burst out toward Winnie and the kids. Ashton jerked his head to the side, scorching the bedroom wall instead of his family.

Winnie and the kids started crying and scrambled as far away from him as they could get. Their bodies grew rigid and their eyes snapped to attention, with a familiar look of terror. They pressed themselves against the wall, as far from Ashton as they could go. The more they scrambled, the more Ashton flamed. And smoked. And bellowed. And roared. Finally, the resort security staff crashed through the front door.

Ashton turned toward the startled security guards and roared, "This is family business! Stay out if it!"

Ashton pushed his way through the door and marched off toward the water. As the security guards watched from the safety of the doorway and his family cringed in the corner of the room, he flapped his mighty wings and flew away.

- 13 -

SIFTING THROUGH THE ASHES

Ashton flew and flew. He flew aimlessly and fast. He flew without thinking. He wasn't thinking about his family. He wasn't thinking about Frank. He wasn't even thinking about where he was going. He was beyond thinking. He just flew.

After hours of frantic flying, Ashton became exhausted and looked for a place to land. As his eyes scoured the vast blue waters below, he realized he had no idea where he was. He was lost. Worse, there was no land in sight.

Ashton started to panic. Little puffs of smoke snaked out of his nostrils. Finally, he spotted land in the distance. As he neared it, he saw it was a beach he did not recognize. Tall buildings dotted the water. Cars buzzed around the buildings and humans covered the beach. This was not good, since Ashton did not want to be seen. He kept distant from the beach, flying parallel to the water's edge until he found a forested area where he could land unnoticed.

He touched down on the beach, folded his wings tight against his body, and crept into the forest. He was relieved to find that the floor of the forest was soft with a bed of pine needles. He laid down to rest, finding a log to rest his head upon. He daydreamed, then dozed off, woke up, and daydreamed some more.

As he moved in and out of awareness, thoughts flitted across the screen of his mind. He saw himself walking along his home beach with Hope, talking through their difficulties, working out how they could both feel safe in their relationship. He saw Frank, bobbing in the canoe, teaching him about flame control. He saw Olivia, and the starfish, and Chief Charley. He heard the beautiful whale songs.

He also saw himself torching the wall in the Dragon Dreams Resort. He saw himself with the Thorny Back Bowlers, trying not to flame up when they teased him about the split he bowled last weekend. He saw himself visiting Winnie in the burn unit, more times than he cared to remember. He even saw himself as a kid, scared of his dad.

He saw Winnie with her arms around the kids, comforting them. And giving him that reproachful look. Again. Then he saw his kids and Winnie cowering in the corner of their room at the resort, their faces masks of terror.

He felt lost. Totally lost. Not just right now, in this forest. But lost in his life. Where had he taken a wrong turn? He thought of himself as a very nice dragon. He knew he had a big heart. But a manly dragon couldn't wear his heart on his sleeve. So he had boxed it up, just as his mom had taught him. And when he let it out a little, hoping to share it with his wife and kids, they didn't want it. They were scared of him.

How had this happened? Why couldn't he just do all of those things that Frank and his friends had taught him?

Ashton knew he was a failure. A no-good dragon. Maybe he would just stay here in this forest forever. The dragons he loved would be better off without him. Ashton closed his eyes again and allowed himself to fall into a deep, troubled sleep.

In his sleep he dreamed. There was a council of sorts. All of the folks he loved were there, sitting in a circle: his mom and dad, his Great Uncle Fernando (the greatest fire-breather of all), Winnie, Phillip and Penny, even Frank. Ashton was in the middle of the circle, sitting on a throne-like chair. They all gathered around him and said, "We love you, Ashton. We want you to be happy. We want you to come home. You are not a failure. You are a normal dragon experiencing life's ups and downs. Just like we are normal dragons and birds and humans. Not one of us is perfect. We all do things to hurt you and to hurt others. And we are all trying to learn to be better. We are all works in progress. So please come back. We can learn from each other and all be better because of each other."

Each of these phrases materialized from the mouth of the speaker like a cloud of beautiful diamond dust. The dust settled on Ashton and on the ground around him. Soon, Ashton shimmered and sparkled like an exotic and beautiful jewel. Ashton felt beautiful. He felt loved. He felt accepted. He felt safe.

In the dream, he felt a slight pressure on his right shoulder. He turned his head, and there was Hope. She was looking into his huge right eye with an impossible amount of love. A joyous tear trickled down Ashton's face. As long as he had Hope, he could do it. He could continue to try to change. He could continue to work on his flame control.

Slowly, Ashton began to wake up. He realized there really was a weight on his right shoulder. He opened his eyes, and there she was. Hope. He sat up, groggy, looking for all of the others who were in his dream. They were not there. As he awakened more fully, he realized the whole thing had to be a dream because his Great Uncle Fernando had passed away when Ashton was a young dragon. And his mom and dad lived very far away. Yet . . . here was Hope. He was so confused he just sat there, saying nothing.

"I thought that was you!" Hope exclaimed. "I saw you from very far away and saw you come into the forest. What are you doing so far from home?"

Ashton sagged against a tree stump and rubbed his eyes.

"I don't even know where home is." Fatigued oozed

from every pore. Ashton hated the thought of telling the whole miserable story. But Hope waited patiently.

"I really messed up. I took the wife and kids over to the Dragon Dreams Resort. I'd planned a wonderful weekend for us. But I lost control of my flame really bad. I was so upset and so embarrassed that I just took off and flew until I was too tired to flap one more wing. So here I am. By the way, where am I?"

Hope explained to Ashton that he was just outside Convention City, a city made up mostly of hotels and conference centers, designed to fulfill its name.

"Too bad that's not where Frank's convention is," Ashton said. "I would sure love to talk to Frank right now."

"Well, you may be in luck," Hope said. "There are some outdoor exhibits over there, and there's an awful lot of stuff that looks like it might be for firemen. I'll bet he's over there somewhere."

Ashton perked up.

"If only I could try to find him. But I'm afraid I would probably scare everyone off. So many people aren't used to seeing dragons. They think we're the stuff of fairy tales, you know."

They sat quietly, lost in their own thoughts.

Then Hope said, "You know, I have really good vision. That's how I find my food in the water. I'll bet I could find Frank. I'll go look for him if you like."

Ashton said he would appreciate that. Hope flew off, and Ashton settled back down into his nest of pine needles. His body felt leaden from the emotional wallop of the day, and he nodded off.

He awoke to the sound of footsteps and voices. He lifted his head and saw Frank and another man coming his way, led by Hope alternately flying and hopping ahead of them. He sat up, excited to see Frank and a little disappointed that Frank had brought someone with him, a tall man with ramrod straight posture and muscular arms wedged into a white T-shirt.

"Ashton," Frank said as he approached, "Hope tells me you have had a recent flame-up that you're feeling terrible about it. She didn't give me a lot of details, but it sounded complicated so I thought I'd bring along my new friend, Ira. He's a forensic fire investigator. He sifts through the ashes of a fire to figure out what started it."

Frank introduced Ira and Ashton to each other. The three sat down on nearby boulders. Frank asked Ashton to please explain to both himself and Ira exactly what had happened.

Ashton told the whole sordid tale, with Frank and Ira nodding occasionally and taking notes. Hope sat next to Ashton, giving him the courage to go on with all of the embarrassing details. When he was finished, Frank looked to Ira.

"Ira, can you figure out what might have caused this flame-up?"

"This is not a simple cause-and-effect situation," Ira said. "I can see many things that all combined led up to such a big fire. Shall we take a look?"

Ashton nodded yes, and Ira began to scrape away the pine needles from a section of the forest floor. When he had a large patch cleared, he picked up a long pointed stick and drew four columns on the ground. He labeled the four columns: THOUGHTS, BEHAVIORS, FEELINGS, and NEEDS.

"As I already said, when an unexpected flare-up like this occurs, there are many contributing factors. I've sorted them out into these categories, and I'd like for you to help me fill in the columns. Let's start with the THOUGHTS column."

Ashton sighed. He was skeptical.

"Okay. I wasn't thinking much, though. I was mostly trying not to let my flame kick in."

"I'm sure you were," Ira said. "On the way over, Frank was telling me what a good student you had been as he taught you flame control and how hard you worked to make changes in your relationships. I wonder, though, if you were so focused on not flaming up that you forgot to pay attention to what you were thinking. Maybe the fog that Frank told you about crept back in?"

"Maybe . . ."

"So," Ira continued, "as you were telling me the story, it sounded like you thought that Winnie and the kids should be excited about the weekend you had planned, is that correct?"

"Yes."

"So that is the first thought I will put here. Do you know what you were feeling when you thought that?"

"Frustrated, because I worked so hard to plan a good trip."

"Okay," Ira said, "I'll put *frustrated* in the FEELINGS column. Now, what did you think when Winnie told you that they were afraid to take this trip with you because of the incident on your last vacation?"

Ashton kicked a rock with his foot.

"I thought they don't appreciate all of the work I've done on my flame control. And I thought that, if they loved me, they'd want to go to Dragon Dreams with me." Ashton hesitated, then said, "Oh, I get it! I also felt hurt that they didn't appreciate my work. And afraid they don't love me anymore."

"Excellent. I'll put those in the two columns."

As Ira wrote the thoughts and feelings down, Ashton's thoughts came quickly.

"Then, when we got to the room at the resort, a couple of things happened. I thought Winnie should control the kids better and that, if she loved me, she should want to watch a movie with me and cuddle on the couch."

"Good," Ira prompted. "And the feelings that went with those thoughts?"

"I was sad that Winnie didn't want to cuddle with me. I was nervous about the kids bickering all week-end—that stresses me out. I don't know how Winnie handles it. I probably even thought I was a bad dad and felt guilty because if Winnie can handle the bickering, I, too, should be able to handle it."

Ira was writing as fast as he could.

"Then, the next morning, I thought that Winnie shouldn't take the kids' side over mine. She should always be on my side. And when they were all complaining, I kept thinking they're a bunch of ingrates."

"And the feelings?"

Ashton thought for a minute. "Unappreciated. Like I said, I worked really hard to find a resort that was family-friendly." He kicked a pine cone with his foot and listened as it skittered across the forest floor. "I just wanted to take a hike, that's all. Don't I get to take a hike with my family?"

Ira knew that was a rhetorical question and didn't bother to answer. Instead he said, "Your awareness is right on, Ashton. I can see why Frank says you are a good student."

"I don't feel like a good student. Don't forget, Dragon Dreams security came to the room."

"Well, I said you're a good student. I didn't say you had graduated yet!" Ira chuckled. His laughter was robust and friendly. "Are there any other things you can think of that should go in these two columns?"

"Yes, one more thing. Well, lots of things, really, but this one seems important. When I tried to check into our room and found out it might be several hours until we could get in, I had a sense of dread. I was nervous about how Winnie and the kids would react. I didn't want to get off to a bad start to a weekend they didn't want to take anyway."

"Good," Ira said, scratching quickly into the dirt. Ira muttered under his breath, " I wish I knew shorthand." Ashton and Frank both smiled but said nothing.

"Okay," Ira said, shaking out his hand and sucking on a blister on his middle finger. "Now it's time to look at the Behaviors column. I know about one big behavior: that would be the flame. What were your other behaviors before the flame-up?"

Ashton paused, thinking.

"Well, I wanted to control everything. I insisted that everyone take this trip, whether they wanted to or not. And then I demanded that everyone get up early to leave. I think I was trying to sway things in my direction by taking over."

"That could be." Ira was writing these things in the Behaviors column. "Very often, when we are feeling a little afraid that things won't go the way we want, we take control to make sure things do go the way we want. Of course, that often backfires."

This sounded right to Ashton. He nodded.

Ira pointed to the final column.

"Frank, what have you taught Ashton about the unconscious purpose of his accidental flare-ups?"

"That they are an attempt to get his needs met. That they're important messengers," Frank said. "In fact, we've used an imaginary decoder ring to find out what the message is behind the flame so that he can find other ways to get his needs met."

"Excellent," Ira said. "Ashton, as you told me the story of what happened at Dragon Dreams, you told me that there were a few times when you felt yourself heating up or saw a little smoke escape. Did you remember to use your decoder ring?"

"No. I was too busy focusing on my family."

"I thought so. That's okay. This is how we learn. So now, looking back, do you know what your needs were?"

Ashton lowered his eyes and looked inside himself. He struggled. He still wasn't very good at feelings. He saw Hope out of the corner of his eye and remembered the long beach walk with Hope. Then everything clicked.

"I do know what I need!" He was so excited, his voice echoed off the tall trees. "I was feeling lonely and scared. My family is so distant from me now. Not that I blame them, but I was feeling unloved. What I need is to feel safe. To feel loved and appreciated. To feel like I belong. To know that my family will be there for me no matter what, just like Hope and Frank."

Ashton let out a long exhalation of relief. Tears stung his eyes as he connected with the knowing that he held deep inside himself. The knowing that Hope and Frank really did care about him—a lot. The knowing that he wanted that from his family, too.

He looked up at Frank and Hope.

"Thank you for being my friends and for loving me. You've taught me that I am lovable no matter how much I mess things up. You've taught me that I can change, and you've helped me change already." Ashton felt like he was wrapped in a soft blanket of his own feelings. "Ira, thank you for helping make sense of the disaster at the resort. I felt so lost before all of you came. Now I have a map. A plan. I will go back home and tell my family how I'm feeling and ask for what I need. I will see if they can forgive me and give me another chance."

Ashton shook hands with Frank and Ira, who left to rejoin their convention. He stayed a few moments more, talking with Hope. Hope gave him directions to get back home, and he took off, each strong flap of his mighty wings carrying him closer to his family

PART IV

- 14 -

Putting the Pieces Together

When he saw his neighborhood in the distance, Ashton felt apprehensive. And embarrassed. His family had seen him at his worst, yet again. He wanted to show them the new, improved Ashton, yet he kept reverting back to the old, out-of-control dragon. *I hope I can keep my flame under control when I get home,* he thought to himself. *This could get ugly. I'll bet everyone is really mad at me.*

He touched down in front of the entrance to his home, took a deep breath, and squeaked open the door. No one was home. He went to the kitchen. It smelled like lemons and the counters sparkled. But Winnie wasn't there.

"Honey?" he called. No answer.

He looked out the back window to see if the kids were in the backyard, but the yard sat empty. He went to the kids' bedrooms. The beds were made and everything looked tidy. Uncharacteristically tidy. No tennis shoes were scattered around the room. No abandoned books. No clothes hastily tossed on the floor.

Ashton's heart began to thud. A wave of grayness passed over him, a dark premonition. Where was his family? He gripped the door of the bathroom and looked inside. A note written on notebook paper was taped to the bathroom mirror. It was in Winnie's crabbed hand-writing. It simply said: "We've gone to my parents." That was it. No idea when, or if, they would be back.

He ran to his bedroom and dropped onto the edge of the bed as if a giant stone were tied around his neck. He felt as if whole sections of his body had been torn away. Putting his great big head in his hands, he sobbed. *I've really done it this time,* he thought. *I've finally lost them!*

After a while, his tears dried. He just sat there, staring at the sage green walls of his bedroom, thinking. He realized he had cried more since he first met Hope than he had in his entire life. Even though he was crying because he felt sad, in some ways it felt good. It felt good to know he was sad and to let himself weep. Surprisingly, he didn't feel like a dragonette at all. In fact, he had decided that only a very manly he-dragon could cry, because in some ways it was easier to leave feelings to the she-dragons than to feel them himself.

Ashton picked up the phone to call Winnie's parents and slowly put the receiver back down without dialing. He leaned against the wall and slowly slid down to the floor. He put his head in his hands and sighed. He knew that Winnie needed a break from his anger. He would give her and the kids the time away from him that they needed. With this thought, another tear trickled down his snout, splashing onto the note from Winnie that he had carried with him. I wish I could get away from myself sometimes, he thought.

As the days passed, Ashton spent a lot of time thinking. After all, his family was gone. His office was closed for the week, so he was not working. There wasn't a lot to do. He let himself think and feel instead of distracting himself with puttering around the house.

He started thinking about his childhood. He was so afraid of his dad. He thought about the times his dad almost burned him with his flame, sometimes he actually got singed. He remembered how he never felt like he fit in at school, because he was different from the other dragons, smarter but less athletic. He thought about how his dad taught him to use his flame when his classmates were picking on him. About how his dad always told him he would never amount to anything. He knew he had spent his whole life trying to prove his dad wrong. He wondered—was his dad proud of him? He never said so.

He thought about how his mom taught him to protect his heart by putting it in a big, thick box. That box had seemed like a good idea at the time, but now he wanted to get rid of it. It weighed him down and got in the way of his relationships. Why did he need to protect his heart from the ones who loved him?

Ashton thought about how he wished his mom would have stood up to his dad when Dad was so cruel. How could she just go to the back of the cave and drink Flame Tamer when Ashton was so scared and vulnerable? Wasn't it a mom's job to protect her children?

At first he felt a tinge of anger at his mom, but the anger quickly turned to sadness. She must have been unhappy, hiding in the back of the cave with her bottle and her dreams. He wondered what she was like when she was young, when she decided to marry his dad. What did she think their future would be like? How close did she get to the life she had hoped for? Not very close at all, he imagined.

He remembered how scared he used to be when his mom would drink so much Flame Tamer that he couldn't wake her up in the morning to fix his breakfast. He remembered packing himself lunch and going off to school, hoping she would be all right. He wished he could have told someone about all of this, but he'd always known it was a very important secret. No one could know about his mom's drinking. No one could know how his dad treated him. No one could know how scared he was inside–and how lonely. No one could know. He even stopped letting himself know. It just hurt too much.

By the time he was a teenage dragon, he was drinking quite a bit of Flame Tamer himself. Funny thing, though, it didn't tame his flame at all. It made it worse. When he was drinking, he would flame up at little things, like when friends teased him about his long tail, or big things, like when his teacher gave him a D on a paper. Sometimes he would drink so much Flame Tamer, he would pass out. He recognized this as the deep sleep his mom used to be in when he was a kid. So, he decided to stop drinking the stuff. He didn't like being so out of control of his flame. He didn't want to be like his dad. He didn't like escaping into the stuff. He didn't want to be like his mom.

Now he realized that even though he didn't want to, he had turned out a lot like both his mom and his dad. He didn't drink, but he could sure escape into his secret cave. And his flame was just as out of control as his dad's, maybe even more so. Turns out, he knew what he didn't want to do, but he didn't know how not to do it.

Until he met Frank. Frank had taught him how to do things differently. How to start unboxing his heart so he could feel. And how to pay attention to his thoughts.

And yet, sometimes his feelings seemed bigger than the situation at hand warranted. When he looked back on some of his biggest flare-ups, he couldn't quite understand why he had gotten as upset as he had, why the feelings he buried in the flame were so strong.

He thought about the things he had hidden in the back of his secret cave. Boxes and boxes were crammed into the cave. Memories were connected to all the items in the boxes. He realized that almost all of the memories were sad memories. *Why,* he wondered, *did I keep all of that stuff?*

He had things in there from his whole life. Even things his mom had saved from when he was a little baby dragon. Almost everything his mom had given him had a story. He realized he had learned from his mom that it was important to remember things that were hurtful so he could keep those painful things from happening again. But it didn't work. He still felt painful feelings.

As he contemplated these things, Ashton realized that life is made up of good times and bad times, happy feelings and sad feelings. Expecting anything else is not realistic. Striving for a life filled with only good things creates a desire for the impossible: constantly feeling happy. The reality is that life is often sad or disappointing.

Ashton's thoughts about his boxes of memories seemed important. The one appointment he had this week was with Frank, and now he was glad. He wanted to talk to him about his stash of stuff.

When Ashton met with Frank, he told him that his family was gone and how frightening that was. He talked about how he was using this time to think about his life—his whole life—and how he had been thinking about the old stuff in his private cave. He told Frank he was pretty sure that stuff was connected to his flame control problems, but he couldn't figure it all out yet.

Frank listened, and then said, "Ashton, you have been doing some deep thinking. You are connecting your past with your present. You are right. The things you learned when you were young and the feelings and stories that you have held onto still live on inside you. They are usually under the surface of your awareness, so you're not really thinking about them. But they affect everything you think and feel.

"It's probably time to start unpacking some of those boxes, going through them, and getting rid of the stuff that isn't helpful to you anymore. The more you can let go of the hurtful things in your past, the more you can really live in the present."

They were in their usual place: Ashton bouncing softly in blue-white ripples of water, Frank bobbing gently in his canoe. Ashton looked down into Frank's face and the sincere expression in his eyes.

"You're right. I'm not even sure what's in about half of those boxes. If I haven't looked in them for so long that I've forgotten what's inside, why do I need them? I think I'll go home right now and start cleaning everything out. Who knows—I might have so much room in the cave that I can turn the whole thing into an artist's studio.

"Someday I'd like to teach the kids the things I have learned from you, and that includes using art projects to figure out what's going on inside."

"That's a great idea. Tell you what, start going through those boxes between now and next week. I'll invite a friend to join us at your secret cave next week. She's a specialist at cleaning out and organizing closets. I'll bet she can help you with anything you haven't finished when we get there."

Ashton thought about it for a minute.

"Terrific. It will be nice to have a female eye. Some of that stuff might be worth keeping for the kids. But I don't know; do they need my old hurtful memories?" Ashton paused, realizing it wasn't a question that could be answered right now. "I'll see what I can get done during the week, then see what your friend says about what would be good to keep and what to get rid of."

"Sounds like you're going to be busy." Frank gripped the wooden paddle of his canoe. "I'll see you next week then. Take care of yourself. There's no telling what you might dredge out of the back of that cave."

As he headed back, Ashton decided it was good that Hope and her friends were gone on a journey up the coast so that he had the cave all to himself. He felt both excited about getting rid of some old stuff and a little nervous about what he might find buried back there. *Well,* he thought, *Frank says it affects me whether I remember it or not. So I may as well remember it.*

At the cave entrance, the scent of moss and pine greeted him. He squared his massive shoulders, took a deep breath, and walked in.

- 15 -

Spring Cleaning the Secret Cave

Standing barely inside the cave, Ashton looked at its contents with a new perspective. There was Hope's nest and all of the little areas he had cleaned out for her flock when they had stayed with him. Good memories and warm feelings flowed over him as he looked at that part of the cave.

His easel and paints and canvases were in the opposite corner. He could smell the piquant aroma of oil mingling with the earthy fragrances in the cave. A canvas sat unfinished with splashes of forest green, burnt orange, and turquoise splattered on it. A stiff painter's brush sat on the edge of the easel, as if it were waiting to be used again. Seeing these, he beamed to himself, remembering his conversations with Hope about his paintings.

Ah, but the rest of the cave. All that stuff! Ashton wasn't sure where to start. He decided to take a quick walk-through and assess the situation, then figure out where to begin. It didn't take long to realize that this idea wasn't going to work. He had jammed so much stuff into the cave that he couldn't even get all the way to the back. *Well, that settles it,* he thought. *I guess I'll just start in the front and work my way back.*

Ashton grabbed the first box he could reach and put it on the ground. He opened the box, which was full of loose papers. What in the world . . .? Ashton could not imagine why this disorganized mess had seemed worth keeping. He pulled up a crate, sat down, and started rifling through the papers. *Oh, yeah,* Ashton thought. *I remember. This is a bunch of papers from work. Old reviews and copies of memos. Each of these papers documents a criticism of my work production. I was saving these in case I ever needed to sue for Wrongful Termination.*

Ashton sat back, thinking. He wondered what Frank would say about this box. Frank would probably ask him how he felt while going through the papers. Figuring out feelings still wasn't very easy for Ashton; however, he was aware that he was heating up inside just looking through these papers. He decided to try to figure out what the heat was connected to.

He realized how hurt he had been by those criticisms at work. He had tried so hard to be the perfect charcoal briquette salesdragon. In fact, his numbers had been better than most of the other dragons' sales numbers. But no matter how hard he tried, he still hadn't pulled in the numbers the bosses wanted. That had made him a little afraid. He'd needed that job to support his family. He felt good that he could identify the pain and fear behind the heat.

He also realized he sometimes felt like a very young dragon when he was being reviewed at work. When he thought about it, he saw the similarities to his childhood. He would try so hard to get his dad's approval, but nothing was ever good enough.

Then Ashton thought to himself, *I get it! Not getting recognized for the things I have accomplished brings up my old, painful feelings from my relationship with my dad. That's why those work situations bothered me so much. That's why my reaction was so much bigger than seemed appropriate. My brain knew I was doing good work and that I wasn't in trouble. I knew that Management always beat up their sales team about numbers. But in my heart, all I knew was that I still wasn't good enough.*

Ashton sat for a few moments, marveling at how his past affected his present. Now that he understood these connections, he didn't want to keep the box of papers. He stood up and dumped the box in a corner at the front of the cave. The papers fell on the floor with a satisfying thud. Even though he felt silly, Ashton said out loud "There! The beginning of the trash pile!" He was surprised at the sound of his own voice. It sounded confident and pleased. He realized he actually *felt* confident and pleased.

As it turned out, that whole section of boxes was connected to his various jobs and the bad feelings he had about those jobs. He happily tossed them all in the trash pile.

By now the sun was dipping beneath the horizon and the sky had turned a muted purple. He had lost track of time. How did it get to be so late? He decided to knock off for the night, thinking, *this is going to be a breeze! I'll be through with this in no time!* He headed up to his home cave, wishing his family would be there but almost glad to have the place to himself. He wanted to spend more time thinking about his career, his dad, and his feelings.

Morning came quickly. Ashton fixed himself a good breakfast. He decided to eat it outside and enjoy the nice spring morning. It was a postcard-perfect day with a primrose sky and scribbles of white clouds. As he ate his oatmeal and fried eggs, birds chirped in the distance. He found himself smiling, enjoying the warbles and peeps and trills. *This is new,* he thought. *In the past the chirping irritated me; now I find it pleasant. I wonder if someday I'll be able to understand what they're saying.*

He headed down to his secret cave, humming, sure he was going to have another easy day of going through boxes and adding them to the trash pile. As he peeked into the cave, his humming stopped. *Gosh,* he thought. *There's still an awful lot of stuff in here. Oh, well, I'd better get at it then.*

Ashton marched resolutely to the boxes toward the back of the cave. He decided to move to a different section of boxes for a change of pace. Confidently, he plucked a box from the top of a stack, sat down on a crate, and opened up the box. The contents took his breath away. Literally. He forgot to breathe for a long while, and then the breath rushed back into him.

Tears welled up in his eyes. In the box were his baby things. His mom had sent them to him years ago when she had gone on one of her cleaning sprees. He had stuck the box in the cave and forgotten it. Until now.

He gingerly lifted out a little pair of baby booties. Blue. Crocheted. With little openings for tiny baby claws to stick out. He wondered, *did my mom make these? For me? We never really talked about when I was a baby. They are so little. It's hard to believe I was ever a baby dragon. It seems like I've been grown up all of my life.*

He held the booties to his chest. He lifted them up to one nostril and sniffed. After all of these years, he could still smell his mom's favorite cologne on them. Just barely. He imagined her, snuggling him up to her chest, telling him how much she loved him and how glad she was that he was her baby dragon. For that instant, he felt loved and special.

Then, without warning, out popped a wisp of smoke. And another. And another. He knew he was angry. Sad. Ashamed. Afraid. All those emotions mixed together.

He couldn't remember his mom ever saying any of those things to him. He would have given anything to remember her really saying some of those things. After all, every little dragon deserves to be loved, and to feel safe.

He slammed the lid back on the box. He just sat there staring at the box. After some time had passed, Ashton picked up the box, walked to the front of the cave, and began a new stack of boxes: the "keep these for now" stack. Resolutely, he walked back to the rear of the cave, picked up another box, and started going through more painful reminders of his past. He wondered where the boxes with the good memories were. Surely he had kept some of that stuff, also?

Days passed. Ashton cleaned through boxes of report cards and yearbooks and certificates. Crates of trophies from his years of playing sports. Tons of awards documenting scholastic and career accomplishments. Pictures of himself, his family, and a few friends. He even found videos of old school plays and choir events.

Each item brought with it forgotten and painful memories. Even the reminders of things he enjoyed, like drama and music, held painful memories for Ashton. His father ridiculed him for his creative endeavors. His mother, an actress herself in her younger days, was drinking so much FlameTamer that she didn't make it to any of his performances.

He spent hours searching through photos, looking for clues about himself and his parents. He didn't have many pictures of himself with friends; close friends were rare for him, both as a child and now. When he looked at the old family photos, he could see that his mother held him a little stiffly. There were no photos of his dad holding him. Over time, he could see his parents standing farther apart in the photos and finally not even being together in the same picture.

As he looked through the boxes, Ashton would slow down and think, and feel, and remember, and imagine. He was beginning to understand himself as he sifted through the reminders of his childhood. Sometimes he felt overwhelmed, and sometimes he felt invigorated. He wanted to call Winnie to share with her what he was learning as he cleaned out his cave. And yet, he didn't. He didn't want to push himself on her. He was beginning to realize how often he insisted things go his way. It seemed right to let her stay with her parents a while longer.

Ashton was aware that he was changing in important ways as he cleaned out his cave. He was grateful for the experience. Still, there was so much stuff! A week had gone by, but piles of boxes were still packed tightly in the cave.

As Ashton was about to decide that it was hopeless, that he could never go through all of the boxes, he heard Frank calling his name from the entrance of the cave. He hurried to the front of the cave, happy to see Frank, embarrassed by the mess he had created in the cave, and shy about meeting Frank's friend.

Frank waited patiently at the door, wearing his usual khaki shorts and T-shirt. With him was a short, plump woman with spiky, blonde-gray hair wearing a silky, watermelon-colored shirt with tiny pearl buttons.

"Ashton, I'd like for you to meet my dear friend Connie. Connie is a closet consultant. She makes her living by helping people go through stuff. Together they decide what to keep and what to throw, and then organize the items that are being kept."

Connie stretched out her hand and said, "Any friend of Frank's is a friend of mine."

As with all of Frank's friends, Ashton felt instantly comfortable with Connie. He gave her a tour of the cave, showing her his small "trash" pile, his small "keep" pile, and his HUGE "I don't know" pile. Connie smiled knowingly.

"I see you have the same problem most of us do. Sometimes it's just hard to know what you want to hang on to. Shall we get started?"

Connie and Ashton began digging through the boxes, discussing the meaning of the items inside and whether they were still of value to Ashton. Often, they consulted with Frank, because of Frank's ability to help decipher the feelings that were connected to many of the things. Frank and Connie helped Ashton to understand that he didn't need to get rid of everything at once. Even getting rid of a some of the stuff would open up a lot of room in the cave.

As darkness came, Frank and Connie prepared to leave. Connie offered to come daily to help Ashton until the cave was completely sorted through. Ashton took her up on the offer, asking Frank if he would mind coming by the cave each week until the project was finished, rather than meeting out in the water. Frank said he thought that was a great idea.

So Connie and Ashton talked, sorted, stacked, and

arranged; unstacked and rearranged. They periodically consulted Frank and moved things around again.

"Keep anything that seems important to you now," Frank said. "You can always get rid of it later."

Ashton found that he was getting rid of a surprising amount of stuff. As more and more things were taken out of the cave and discarded, Ashton found himself feeling less and less cluttered inside. It was as if he were not only cleaning out his cave but also cleaning out his heart and mind. Ashton knew that he was creating space in his cave for the art studio he wanted to set up for his kids, and that he was also creating space inside his heart to store happy memories.

The last thing Ashton went through was the emergency supply pack that he kept near the cave entrance. In addition to a fire extinguisher and first aid supplies, the pack contained gifts to give to those in his life after he hurt them. He remembered the time that he had bought diamond wing accents for Winnie after a big flame-up. He knew now that he had given gifts as a form of insurance, so those he cared about would forgive him for his flame-ups and still be a part of his life.

Ashton decided that in the future he would use his communication skills instead of gifts to repair relationship damage. He boxed up the gifts to give to charity and put together a small pack with first aid supplies and a fire extinguisher. *After all,* Ashton thought, *accidents can still happen, whether or not my flame is involved.*

Finally, Connie and Ashton were finished. When Frank came for his weekly visit, the cave was transformed. Neatly arranged shelves of boxes and photo albums were in the back of the cave. A couple of shelves were stacked with open boxes filled with sand and moss—nesting places for Hope and her friends when they came to visit. The rest of the cave was open with easels and canvases and art supplies throughout: a true artists' lair.

Warm, yellow sunlight filtered through the cave. A few small openings had been uncovered that were sheltered enough on the outside to keep out the rain, yet allowed the sunshine to come in. The light bathed the interior with a homey, welcoming feeling, enriched by the earthy, clean scents of the cave. Frank, Ashton, and Connie admired the cave together, impressed with the work they had done.

Ashton thanked Connie for her help, and he and Frank arranged their meeting on the water for the following week. Frank and Connie left the cave together, while Ashton surveyed his cave one more time, enjoying a wonderful sense of comfort. He moved around the cave, brushing his fingers across his paintings, sniffing the fresh air coming through the holes in the roof, and admiring his orderly shelves. He felt more content and happy and just plain old good than he could remember feeling in a long time.

As he began his walk back home, Ashton started to review his time with Frank and thought about how much his life had changed. There had been hard times, sad times, and painful times. Still, the end result was all worth it. Ashton was truly beginning to understand his flame. And with understanding came control.

He only hoped that somehow he could get one more chance with Winnie and the kids.

- 16 -

Painting Circles

For several days after completing his cave clean-out, Ashton felt at loose ends. The cave project had consumed him for weeks. It had been physically and emotionally exhausting, and it was probably the most rewarding thing he had ever done. Yet now that the project was completed, he had time on his hands.

Work filled his days, but the evenings were lonely. It had been several weeks since Winnie and the kids left. He had thought he would hear from them, but he hadn't. He wanted to call them, but he had no idea what to say. So he decided not to, at least not yet. He hadn't seen Hope in a while either; she and her friends must have found a lovely spot to visit for a while.

When the weekend came, Ashton decided to go to the secret cave and try painting. He stood in the cave and looked around. He breathed deeply. His scales tingled. Important things had happened here, he knew.

He also knew that right now he had only the slightest understanding of how important some of those things were. All he knew was that he was a changed dragon. He saw the world differently. He saw himself differently. He wondered—would the world see him differently? Would they notice all the changes that had taken place inside of him? As he thought about these changes, he realized it really didn't matter if anyone else noticed or not. The changes were there, and he was happy, and that was the most important thing.

Ashton walked over to an easel and started dabbing paints on a canvas: golden shades of yellow, bright hues of purple and green. As he painted, he thought about Winnie and the kids. He wanted so badly to see them. He still hadn't contacted them. In the past, he had always pushed himself on them, even when they needed space away from him. Now he knew that he had been scared they would stop loving him and wanting him around. He understood that he'd tried to be with them all the time and control what they did so he could force them to love him. Of course, this ultimately drove them away.

Ironic, he thought to himself. *I tried so hard to not be alone that I ended up being alone. But it was while I was alone, and with Frank and Connie and Hope that I learned to start letting go of the past. And to stop seeking everyone else's approval. And to see that I really am a good dragon. When I stopped trying to be perfect, I stopped being so imperfect. Funny how that works. I wonder if now that I've stopped chasing Winnie and the kids, is it possible that they might come back to me?*

As he painted, he thought about Winnie, the kids, and Hope. He also thought about Frank and their time together. Although he had a few things to talk to Frank about, he didn't feel as desperate to see Frank as he used to. *Perhaps I will talk to Frank about that, too,* Ashton thought. *Maybe Frank has taught me enough about flame control for now.*

Ashton was so busy thinking about everything else, the paintbrush sort of painted without him. He finished one canvas and started another. Finally, he put his brush down and stepped back. He looked at his painting of three circles. *What in the world is that?* he thought. *Hmm . . . Hope is not here to help me decipher this one. I'll have to do it myself.*

He pulled up a crate and sat down. He contemplated the circles. He wondered what they could mean. One circle was inside the other. The last circle was outside the other two. They were all touching. It looked familiar . . .

"I know!" His booming voice startled him. He hadn't meant to speak out loud, but he was so excited. "It's me!" A rush of warmth welled up inside him. Not like a fire of white-hot coals, but happy and cozy. A big tear dropped out of each big, dark eye. "It's me, now, all grown up, holding the younger, more tender me, on my lap. Hugging myself. Keeping myself safe. Letting myself know I am always here, and it will all be okay." He stared at his painting in amazement. It summarized all the work he had done with Frank and his friends. His flame-control training was largely about learning to take care of himself. When he felt safe and loved, he could then be there for others. He took one last look at the painting, heaved a contented sigh, and left the cave to take a long walk on the beach.

Lost in thought, Ashton kept his eyes on the sand in front of him. Walking methodically, rhythmically, he followed the high tide line. He didn't even notice when a tiny seagull began flying just behind him. It was only when he stopped to sit on a log and the bird settled down beside him that he realized he wasn't alone.

"Hope! Where did you come from?"

"I've been following you for miles. You looked so lost in thought I didn't want to disturb you."

"I was lost in thought," Ashton acknowledged. "It's been an interesting several weeks since I last saw you."

Hope looked at Ashton for a moment, and then looked out into the water. Dragon and seagull sat together quietly, comfortably, contemplating the vastness of the ocean, and life, and all of those things that one contemplates when hanging out in a beautiful place with a special friend.

Finally Ashton said, "Hope, I can't wait 'til you see the cave. You won't recognize it!" He explained the process of going through the cave with Connie and Frank.

Hope puffed out her chest and her eyes flickered with joy.

"I look forward to seeing the cave. It sounds like the clean-up was a good process for you."

"I have an area set up for you and your friends. It will be a warm, dry spot during the rain. Of course, if you have somewhere else you would like to stay, I understand."

"We'd love to take you up on your hospitality. Sometimes no matter how far we fly, we just can't seem to find a good spot." Hope brushed a gray wing across his cheek. "You're a good friend, Ashton."

Ashton sat quietly, believing her. He knew she considered him a real friend. An important friend. He also knew she would feel this way even if he didn't invite her to stay in his cave. It was him she liked, not what he did.

"Hope, I'm confused about something," Ashton finally said. "Maybe talking it over with you will help me get some direction."

"Of course."

Ashton began to talk about all the things he had learned about himself and about the painting he had just completed. He talked about how badly he wanted to see Winnie and the kids just because he wanted to see them, not because he needed to see them to feel good about himself. He told Hope of his decision not to contact Winnie, because he didn't want her to feel pressured into seeing him. He said he didn't know what to do next. How long should he wait? What if she never contacted him? What if she was waiting for him to contact her?

"You know," Hope said after a while, "these things have a way of taking care of themselves. Why don't you give Winnie a couple more weeks, and then if you don't hear from her, you could send her a note and let her know that you'd just like to see her for lunch or something. That way, she has a chance to see how she feels when she is with you instead of feeling like she needs to decide right away what she's going to do."

"That's a good idea," Ashton said. "I think I'll try that."

Ashton and Hope went back to the secret cave, where Hope acknowledged all of the work he had done. When she saw the new painting, she cocked her head to the side and studied it.

"You know, that painting is so straightforward and balanced. It seems whole. It is simple and perfect. It seems to sum up the transformation you have experienced. When I met you, you were confused, out of control, and hurt. Now you seem solid, balanced, and happy. What a tremendous difference."

"It really is," Ashton said thoughtfully. "I feel so different than when I first met you. I'm the same dragon, but not the same. If you would have told me then what

I would be like now, I would have told you that you were crazy. Yet here we are, a dragon and a seagull, in a comfortable cave, filled with art, talking about life. It doesn't get much better than this."

Hope visited a while longer, then said good-bye to Ashton. Ashton headed to his home cave for the evening. He wanted to rest up. Tomorrow was going to be a big day. It would be his first water visit with Frank in a long time. He wanted to be rested. The day felt important for some reason.

- 17 -

A BARGE FULL OF SURPRISES

The next day, as he flew out to his meeting place with Frank, Ashton realized he had gotten everything he needed from Frank, at least for now. This meeting felt like good-bye. Ashton felt both happy and sad as he thought about this. He would talk to Frank, ask him a few questions, and mostly thank Frank for everything he had done for him. He hoped Frank would be willing to meet with him from time to time, but Ashton thought the need for weekly visits had come to an end.

Frank was already at the designated spot, looking small in his little canoe. Ashton landed beside him, and they began to talk. Frank agreed that it seemed as though their work together was drawing to a close. Frank told Ashton how honored he was to know Ashton and to be able to help him learn flame control.

"I've learned so much more than just flame control," Ashton said, fighting back tears. "I've gotten to know myself, and to accept myself, and to accept others. I couldn't have done it without you."

They discussed their future together. Frank assured Ashton that he was always welcome to come and talk with him. He would be able to see his canoe in the usual spot at the usual time. They decided that if for some reason Ashton needed Frank at a different time, he would ask Hope or one of the other seagulls to find Frank for him. They had a plan, and Ashton felt at peace. Ashton was just about to say good-bye for now, when Frank had one more question.

"Are you up for one more field trip?"

Ashton didn't even have to think about it.

"Of course. I've come to enjoy your field trips. Where are we going?"

"It's a surprise! Just follow me!"

Frank began rowing along the coast, down toward the harbor. As he reached the shipping channel, he turned away from shore and out toward the ocean. Ashton couldn't imagine where they were headed. Then, he heard sounds coming from the middle of nowhere. Music was playing lively melodies, a mix of calypso, steel drums and voices. Laughter rang out between the musical notes. The wonderful smell of sizzling fajitas and burgers sailed through the air on an ocean air current.

They approached a huge barge. Orange and yellow streamers ruffled in the breeze and electric-blue paper umbrellas decorated the sides of the barge. Frank pulled up beside the barge and climbed up a ladder to the deck.

When Ashton landed next to Frank, out rushed all sorts of creatures yelling "Surprise!"

There were humans, dragons, and seagulls. Whales jumped out of the water and splashed the deck. Groups of otters bobbed in the water clapping their paws. Dragons from the bowling league crowded around a barbecue grill, holding enormous multicolored beverages studded with limes and lemons. Seagulls fluttered around a table loaded with bowls of chips, trays of roasted red peppers, and platters of chocolate chip cookies. Ashton was astounded. Was all of this for him?

Then, Winnie and the kids pushed through the crowd. Ashton couldn't believe his eyes. Winnie looked beautiful, her pink scales smooth and shiny. The kids each held a cookie. Phillip's face was smudged with chocolate. They'd never looked better to Ashton.

Nervously, he stood there, not knowing what to do. When they reached him, Winnie and the kids hugged him.

"We've missed you so much," Winnie said.

"Daddy, do you like my new necklace? I got it just for this party," Penny said.

Ashton started crying, big dragon tears splashing on the kids' heads. Wiping away his tears, Ashton asked, "What are you doing here? How did you get here? What is all of this?"

Winnie's wings trembled a bit with anticipation.

"A little birdie told us about this party." She smiled feebly at her attempt at humor. "Yesterday Hope came to visit me and told me that you had been working very hard to control your flame and that you were a changed dragon. She said that you had made friends with a fireman named Frank, who wanted to throw a graduation party for you, and that we were invited. So here we are."

Ashton kissed Winnie on the cheek. He felt shy, like a teenager on a date.

"You've made a lot of good friends I didn't know about." Winnie smiled at him warmly and reached out to hold his hand. "I must say, they are a very interesting batch of creatures!" Just as Winnie finished speaking, Frank stepped up to a microphone, tapping it to break up the conversation.

"May I have everyone's attention? As you all know, we are here today to celebrate Ashton's completion of flame control training. Ashton, could you please join me at the microphone?"

Suddenly overcome with a variety of emotions, Ashton walked slowly up to the microphone. He looked out at the sea of faces: feathered, scaled, furry, human. Frank continued his greeting.

"It is my great honor to award this Certificate of Completion. Ashton, you've done a tremendous amount of work. You have not only learned tools to control your flame, you have looked back into yourself and your history to find out where those sudden bursts of flame come from. You've developed a deep understanding of yourself and those you love. It has been a great pleasure for me to be able to guide you on your journey."

Frank handed the certificate and the microphone to Ashton. It took Ashton several moments to speak. Tears kept spilling out of his eyes and jamming up his throat. Finally he spoke.

"I don't know what to say. You have all become so important to me. So many of you have shared parts of yourself with me, to help me learn about myself. Each of you has helped me in ways that you can never imagine. I am so glad to know you as teachers, mentors, friends, and family. Thank you for being in my life."

Ashton handed the microphone back to Frank. He went back to Winnie and the kids and hugged them. The ceremony was long and happy. The microphone was handed around, as creatures great and small talked about Ashton and told stories, serious and funny, impressive and embarrassing, about the dragon they were here to celebrate.

Ashton worked his way through the crowd, stopping often to say "thank you." He thanked Ira, the forensic fire investigator, for helping him when he was feeling so lost and confused after the big flame-up at the Dragon Dreams Resort. He thanked Charley the Fire Chief for all of the fire safety information, especially the part about the bad wiring. Ashton told Charley about how he had cleaned out his secret cave, which seemed to him a lot like tearing out old, dangerous electrical wires.

Ashton found Connie and thanked her again for all of her help in cleaning out his secret cave. He told her about the painting he had just finished and that he knew the painting had come from all of the work they had done together.

Then Ashton leaned over the side of the barge to talk to Olivia and her friends. He told her how much he had learned about trust from her. And about playfulness. And that it's okay to not be so serious all of the time.

Finally, Ashton took a short flight out over the water. He flew over the whales, dipping each wing toward them in a thankful salute. He wished that others could know about the beautiful songs the whales sang to each other. He realized how lucky he had been to hear their music.

At last it was time for Ashton to leave. He said his good-byes and then went up to Winnie and the kids.

"Is it okay if I call you sometime soon?" he asked.

"There's really no reason," Winnie said with a playful tone to her voice. "We'd like to go home with you."

"Really?!" Ashton couldn't believe his ears. Even though she had been nice to him during the party, he hadn't dared to believe that she was ready to come home. He had been afraid she was going to say there was no reason for them to come home with him because they were leaving him for good.

"Frank arranged for some of his friends to take our luggage back to the cave while we've been here. Everything is there, ready for us to move back in. I hope that is okay with you."

"Okay?" Ashton gasped. "Of course it's okay! I have my family back!"

Ashton got so excited he almost knocked a couple of seagulls over with his tail. They didn't mind, though, because they could hear what was being said. They were happy for him.

Ashton, Winnie, Phillip, and Penny spread their mighty wings and flew away into the evening sky, heading for home. Behind them, Hope and a few friends followed, heading for a restful night in the not-so-secret cave. Everyone knew that important things had happened and that in some small way the world was a better place.

They knew friends had been made.

That the past had been forgiven.

And that all was well.

THE END...and a NEW BEGINNING

ABOUT THE AUTHOR

After receiving her Bachelor of Fine Arts degree, Sheila Hatcher was an Interior Designer/Project Manager in contract settings. In her years in this field, Sheila noticed that she cared much more about how her customers felt in their new spaces than about how "design-perfect" the completed job was. She enjoyed working in boardrooms and on construction sites; her happiest days were days she got to interact with and know people from various walks of life and with vastly different worldviews. Over time, Sheila knew that her life's work was to talk with people and help them make positive changes in their lives.

Sheila graduated with an M.A. in Counseling Psychology from Pacifica Graduate Institute in 2001. Her studies at Pacifica focused on Depth Psychology, which acknowledges the importance of symbol and metaphor in how we view ourselves and our world.

Sheila has extensive experience working with addictions, anger, and depression. She helps her clients tune into their unconscious fears and longings by paying attention to the images which present themselves in session.

Sheila has given many presentations and workshops to the general public and mental health professionals on working with anger and with using symbol and metaphor to reach a deeper understanding of the internal world. She has served as an Adjunct Professor at California State University, Dominguez Hills, and has mentored and supervised professionals new to the field.

For speaking engagements, write to Sheila Hatcher at

25500 Hawthorne Blvd. #1220
Torrance, CA 90505

or E-mail
Sheila@ConnectionsCounselCtr.com

Website: ConnectionsCounselCtr.com

ABOUT THE ILLUSTRATOR

Tianlu Chen is a product designer and active painter working in oil and watercolor. He studied academic classic painting. Tianlu is best known for his genre painting of landscape and architecture. His artworks have been collected by many international influential private art collectors.

Tianlu is a member of the Oil Painters of America and National Watercolor Society. He also lectures on oil and watercolor painting.

Tianlu lives in Los Angeles, California, USA.

www.tianlustudio.com

— To Order —

Sheila Hatcher
25500 Hawthorne Blvd. #1220
Torrance, California 90505
www.ConnectionsCounselCtr.com
E-mail: Sheila@ConnectionsCounselCtr.com
(Connections Counseling Center)

Checks and credit cards accepted

or contact
LangMarc Publishing
P.O. Box 90488
Austin, Texas 78709
For quantity discounts call 1-800-864-1648
E-mail: langmarc@booksails.com
www.langmarc.com

CPSIA information can be obtained
at www.ICGtesting.com
Printed in the USA
BVHW04s1841050918
526615BV00012BA/70/P